The Search
for Ancestors
A Swedish-American
Family Saga

H. Arnold Barton

Southern Illinois University Press
Carbondale and Edwardsville
Feffer & Simons, Inc.
London and Amsterdam

Library of Congress Cataloging in Publication Data

Barton, Hildor Arnold, 1929–
    The search for ancestors.

    Includes bibliographical references and index.
    1. Swenson family. 2. Barton family. 3. Barton, Hildor Arnold,
1929– 4. Sweden—Genealogy. I. Title.
CS71.S9776 1979   929'.2'0973   78-15537
ISBN 0-8093-0893-2

Jorden gömmer, världen glömmer.
[The earth hides, the world forgets.]

Inscription formerly over the gate
to Lost Grove Cemetery

Contents

Preface

The story that follows is threefold. It is the account of my own personal odyssey into the past in search of my Swedish-American pioneering heritage. As such it shows something of the ways in which a search of this kind may be carried on. At the same time it traces an inner voyage of self-discovery.

It is meanwhile an essay in family history, the family being that of my paternal grandfather, which migrated from the province of Småland in Sweden to Iowa in the United States in stages during the 1840s, 1850s, and 1860s, and found new homes in the New World.

Finally, the study of this family reveals the broader contours of Swedish history in the eighteenth century and both Swedish and American history in the nineteenth, in particular those social, economic, and cultural developments that led to the gradual breakup of an ancient way of life in the Swedish countryside and the migration of growing numbers of Swedish peasants across the Atlantic to America. It is a macrocosm in microcosm.

Those of us who concern ourselves with migration history often come up against certain problems of approach. For a migration to be historically significant, it must involve relatively large numbers of people. Yet as part of a mass phenomenon the individual migrants become the objects of statistical analysis and broad generalizations, thus losing their identity as actual men and women faced with the profound human dilemmas that migration imposes. On the other hand, to study only a single migrant in isolation must involve circumstances so unique to that individual as to provide only limited insights into the situations of others. The study of smaller groups of persons, somewhere between the individual and the mass, can meanwhile give a broader view of the historical development without sacrificing the human element. A family—particularly a large one—provides in important respects an ideal unit for a study of this kind and in my grandfather's family, from at least the mid-seventeenth century on, I am fortunate in having one well suited to this purpose.

Migration history also generally tends to consist either of *emigration* or of *immigration* history, but rarely both in combination. In the first instance, it deals with the conditions in the old country that ultimately lead up to the migrant's departure, after which he disappears from the scene; in the latter, the story begins with the migrant's appearance on American soil, essentially a man or woman without a past, whose task it is to assimilate and find a useful role in the new society. The family here under study illustrates equally the histories of both the old country and the new, while revealing something of that long continuity in the life of a family that is as essential in its development as the influences different cultures brings to bear upon it.

While a great many persons have given generous and valuable help in the preparation of this book, as witnessed in both text and notes, the following deserve special mention.

My late father, Sven Hildor Barton, and his sister, Margit McNulty, now of Laguna Hills, California, gave me that fund of family lore which inspired my search and supplied its necessary points of departure. Others in this country to whom I owe particular thanks include Marie Anderson, Gowrie, Iowa; Joel W. Lundeen, Chicago; Rose Mele, Des Moines; Ardith K. Melloh, Iowa City, Iowa; Nils William Olsson, Sumner, Maryland; Kevin Proescholdt, Ames, Iowa; Lilly and Lennart Setterdahl, East Moline, Illinois; Clifford Swenson, Gowrie; and Crayton M. Watkins, Jr., Burbank, California.

In Sweden, sincere thanks go to Eddy Gustafsson, Vimmerby; Gösta Karlsson, Djursdala; Elsa Larsson, Odensvi; Maja Nestor, Södra Vi; Arne Nilsson, Kisa; Kerstin Olsson, Södra Vi; Elsa Östblom, Vadstena; and Albin Widén, Bromma.

I am most grateful to Lucille Vechiarella and Lorie Zaleskas for their careful typing of the manuscript.

My wife, Aina, has been my good and helpful companion

throughout my lengthy search through times past and through strangely contrasting landscapes.

Finally, one person deserves recognition above all others: my kinswoman, friend, and indispensable collaborator in this venture, Karin Augustinson of Ödeshög. Without her, the results of my research would have been modest at best. A good part of this book is as much hers as it is my own. To her it is dedicated with warm gratitude and affection.

H. A. B.

Carbondale, Illinois

April 1978

The Search for Ancestors
A Swedish-American Family Saga

1

Prologue: The Search

When we were children, growing up in California, Dad used to sit on our beds in the evenings and tell stories in the dark. He was a masterful storyteller and he had all kinds of strange and wonderful things to relate. Sometimes he recounted his own experiences. At times he told of what he had heard from his mother about her childhood in northern Sweden. And sometimes he talked about his father, Dr. Ernest Barton, and his family.

Grandfather was also Swedish. His name was originally Ernst Svensson.[1] He was born on Bullebo farm, near a town called Vimmerby in the province of Småland in southern Sweden, and he was one of the eleven children of the farmer Sven Svensson. Sven's wife, whose name Dad could not recall, was the daughter of one "Captain Öhrn," about whom Dad had some remarkable stories to tell; her mother came from a family of church organists. According to Dad, Öhrn was the first in the family to go to America—"very early"—and it was through his success there, Dad was convinced, that his son-in-law, Sven, with wife and eleven children, immigrated to Iowa around the time of the Civil War. Here Sven acquired a large tract of virgin land on the prairie. Dad once said, while we were working in the vegetable garden, that he supposed he must by now be related to half the people in western Iowa. As the Swedes were not very attached to the names ending in -*son*, since each generation in a family simply added it to the father's Christian name, several of the Svenssons changed their names. Grandfather eventually became Barton; Dad meanwhile seemed to recall that several of the others had taken the name West.

Grandfather Ernest had apparently not thrived in the strict religious atmosphere of the family home and eventually went to Augustana College in Rock Island, Illinois. Later he went to the University of Nebraska Medical School in Omaha. It was while he was there that he heard the traveling "Swedish Ladies' Quartette" and met its leading soprano, Jenny Norelius. It was love at first sight. They were soon married and moved to Portland, Oregon, where Ernest set up his medical practice and where my father, Sven Hildor Barton, was born in 1892 and his sister, Margit, in 1896.

To all of this I listened with rapt attention and what I heard I would not forget; I can still remember many of the things he told about his family in the very words he used. It was surely at this time that I discovered I possessed the instincts of the historian. From time to time I questioned Dad further about his father and family. Often he was unable to answer. He had left home too early in life. He knew too little about his parents' backgrounds and what he recalled was on some points confused and misleading. Yet it would prove ample enough, when the time came, to start me off on my own odyssey into the past. In the meantime I became fascinated with things Swedish and throughout my earlier teens read everything on Sweden and Scandinavia I could lay my hands on. I resolved, too, that I would learn the ancestral language at the first chance.

That opportunity came already in 1948–49, when I was eighteen, the year after I finished high school, when my family visited Europe. After Christmas in Stockholm, we spent several weeks in midwinter in Grandmother Jenny's native village in the province of Hälsingland, where we were able to learn much about her and her background. By the time I left I had acquired a solid enough foundation in Swedish that I could continue to use it and improve upon it in the years ahead. We did not, however, visit the Vimmerby region, where Grandfather Ernest and his family had come from. I can only regret that we did not, for there were people then still living there who could have told us much that we now can never know. In Dad's notebook from that trip, which I acquired after his death in 1972, there are notations about the Svenssons and the Vimmerby area which show both that he probably hoped to go there at the time and that he somehow knew certain bits of information which he obviously forgot in his later years and which I was only able to rediscover with considerable effort when I began my own search.

Some eight years passed, filled with other interests, during which time I went to college and served in the U.S. Coast Guard, aboard ships in the Mediterranean and the Pacific. After getting out of the military I prepared, in the summer of 1957, to drive east to Princeton University in New Jersey, where I was to enter graduate school. It occurred to me that since my route would go through Iowa I might well take the opportunity to discover whether we had any Svensson relatives still living there. Dad had never been there and had never had any personal contact with anyone there. He could not even recall the name of the community, although he knew it was somewhere near Fort Dodge. The situation was saved by his sister, my Aunt Margit, who remembered that it was Gowrie. Thus prepared, I set off, together with my sister Barbara, who kept me company across the Continent.

On a late summer Sunday morning we found our way into Gowrie, Iowa. Church was over and the streets were deserted. We were not sure where to start. We tried unsuccessfully to find the Lutheran pastor. An older man passed by in the elm-shaded street. We stopped him and asked if he had ever heard of anyone called West in the area. He shook his head. When we explained that the family had originally been Svensson and that our grandfather had become a doctor and had gone out west, this seemed to ring a bell. After consulting with a local matron on her screen porch, he came back and informed us that the people we were looking for must be the Swensons, whose farm was about a mile south of town. Our informant spoke with so noticeable a Swedish accent that I asked him where he came from. Right here, he replied. We realized that we were somewhere close to the heart of Swedish America.

The Swensons were assembled on the porch of the white frame farmhouse, following Sunday dinner. There was Dad's first cousin, old Theodore Swenson, then close to eighty, with his sweeping handlebar mustaches, and his wife, Selma, both of them frail and white-haired. There too was their son, Clifford, the present farmer on the place, his wife, Lucile, and their three young children. It took no more than a few words of explanation on our part and everything quickly fell into place: we were the long-lost relatives from California. We were welcomed in a hearty yet thoroughly natural way, as though we had somehow been expected to show up eventually.

Theodore told various things about the family. It was true that one or two of the first generation had taken the name West, but others had called themselves Westerdal or Westerdale, and one respelled the family name Swainson, to make it seem more "American." "Your grandfather took the name Barton," he said with a glint in his eye; "Thought it sounded fancier!" They had not all settled down as farmers in Gowrie, as old Sven Svenson had hoped, but had scattered all over the country. One became a clergyman and eventually went back to Sweden. Another had served in the Civil War. "On which side?" Barbara asked naïvely. The old man drew himself up to his full height. "On the *right* side," he replied with simple dignity. He showed us the old guest book where Grandfather Ernest had written a bit of doggerel verse about picking corn and a memorable turkey dinner during a visit in 1902.

Clifford Swenson then took us a mile or two down the road to the east to visit Dad's only other cousin still living around Gowrie, Mrs. Marie Anderson, who lived alone on what was left of Sven Svenson's original farm. She too was delighted to see us. But it was by now well into the afternoon and we had to continue on our way. It would be sixteen years before I would see Clifford Swenson and his family and Marie Anderson again. By the time I next returned to Gowrie, in 1973, old Theodore and Selma were long gone.

The sequel to this visit was that contact was established between Clifford Swenson and my parents and aunt. They corresponded and a year or two later Clifford visited them in California. In this way Dad was able to learn more about his father's family. In the summer of 1960, Mother and Dad visited Sweden for the second time. They went to Vimmerby and there were able to find that Bullebo farm was located in Djursdala parish, some ten kilometers to the north. There they visited with the present owners, Nils and Maria Olsson, and Dad spoke to various people in the neighborhood and picked up some details which he later passed on to me. On the return trip across the United States by car, Mother and Dad also visited the Swensons in Gowrie.

More years would now pass. I completed my doctoral studies at Princeton, developing a special research interest in Scandinavian history. In 1960 I began my university teaching career at the University of Alberta, in Edmonton, Canada, and during that Christmas vacation flew to Stockholm to marry Aina Margareta Bergman in the twelfth-century church of her native Solna. My knowledge of Sweden's history and language grew over the years, although I as yet had no chance to get into the subject of Swedish immigration to America.

In 1966, when we were in Sweden on sabbatical leave, we visited Djursdala and Bullebo farm. Looking for the farm, we stopped to ask the way of an old man who was pushing his bicycle along the side of the road. He was, of course, interested in who we might be. I explained that my great-grandfather, Sven Svensson, had been the farmer at Bullebo, which he had sold about a hundred years ago when he had left with his family for America. Without batting an eyelid the old fellow thereupon informed me that a relative of mine had just died, only a few days before. I was so taken aback that I did not even think to ask who that might have been. This was my first, striking experience of how long memories linger on in "darkest Småland," as they say in Sweden. It would not be the last time.

The Olssons were not home at the old home farm. Instead we visited with Erik and Astrid Karlsson on the neighboring farm to the north, a part of the old Bullebo lands, they told us, that had gone to Sven Svensson's brother, Carl Johan, in the town of

Horn, through the division of their father's inheritance in 1854. Carl Johan had also gotten the old farmhouse at Bullebo, which he had transported and reassembled in Horn. Thus Sven Svensson's family had lived in a smaller wing building. Erik Karlsson showed us around his own place. At the barn, during evening milking, we met his two sons before continuing over to the neighboring Olsson farm, which one of them leased and cultivated. My feelings upon treading these ancestral acres and entering the farmyard with its ancient, red-painted, timbered outbuildings and the modest two-storied house where my grandfather was born, can well be imagined. The summer twilight gathered and we had to move on. By the side of the road as we entered Horn we caught a glimpse of the old "big house" which Carl Johan Svensson had moved from Bullebo.

Later that same year, while doing research in Stockholm, I decided to seek out actual documentation of the Svenssons' emigration. I was directed to the immense block-long Statistical Central Bureau and within no time at all held in my hands the pastors' annual statistical summaries for Djursdala from the mid-1860s on. But when had the family come over? Was it in 1869, as my father had seemed to recall, or 1867, as my aunt claimed? Under the year 1867 I quickly found what I was looking for among the list of emigrants from the parish to "North America" on the back of the report. Among the twenty-eight emigrants for that year were "former farm-owner" Sven Svensson, born 1817, his wife Maria Örn, born 1823, and eight children, with years of birth. These data were indispensable. But I had always heard that there were eleven children in the family. One case seemed clear: if one son had served in the Civil War he would have had to go over earlier than the rest of the family. The same was thus probably true of the other two who were not accounted for. Among the nine emigrants for the previous year, 1866, I did note a "student," Sven Fredrik Westerdal, who also came from Bullebo farm, but I did not understand the connection. Emigrants were not listed by name for years earlier than 1865.[2]

Here the search ended, for the time being, while I devoted

myself to the history of eighteenth-century Sweden. We had been living since 1963 in Santa Barbara, California, where I taught at the University of California. In 1970 I took a position at Southern Illinois University in Carbondale. Right at that time I also accepted an invitation from the Swedish Pioneer Historical Society to prepare an annotated anthology of Swedish immigrant letters from America.[3] Both these developments were of decisive importance for the search for the Svenssons' family history which I had carried on in such desultory fashion for so long, in a sense since childhood: we were now living in the Midwest, not far from localities associated with the family's past and I likewise had compelling reasons to devote myself seriously to the study of Swedish-American history.

In the summer of 1971 we were again in Stockholm, where I came across two more useful sources of information. The emigration historian, Albin Widén, when I visited him at home in Bromma, pulled out of his shelves a slim paper-covered volume on the Swedish settlements in western Illinois and Iowa.[4] To my delight, the section on Gowrie gave a good deal of information on the prominent Svenson family of that community. Some of the details I later discovered to be mistaken and misleading. But I now knew far more about the Svensons in Iowa than before. Among other things, this source confirmed that the eldest son of the family, Sven Fredrik Westerdal, whose name I had noted on the Djursdala list of emigrants for 1866, had been a pastor in the Augustana Lutheran Church but had later returned to Sweden, where he died "as a minister in the state church."[5] This detail led me to a second useful source, the biographical dictionaries for the clergy of the various Swedish dioceses. Skimming through the indexes of several of these, I found S. F. Westerdal in one of the volumes for the Härnösand diocese in northern Sweden, which contained valuable details on his life and work.[6]

With these additional materials in hand I returned to Carbondale and right after Christmas 1971 took the big plunge by sending long lists of questions to Dad, Aunt Margit, Clifford Swenson in Gowrie, and the farmer Erik Karlsson, Djursdala. Neither

Dad nor Aunt Margit was able to add very much to what I had already heard from them, as I had expected, though Aunt Margit did provide a deft character sketch of her father, Ernest. Clifford Swenson, in consultation with Marie Anderson, provided a wealth of information about the various members of the Svenson family. From Djursdala came a reply, not from Erik Karlsson but from his son, Gösta, whom we had met so briefly in 1966; this would be the beginning of an intensive and highly rewarding collaboration during the next two years, for Gösta turned out to be a natural-born historian. I spent long days at the typewriter, formulating questions. Soon too, I sent inquiries to the Vadstena *landsarkiv*, or provincial archive, where church, property, and other official records from northeastern Småland are kept, and to *Riksarkivet*, the National Archives in Stockholm, for more information about Pastor Westerdal. Scarcely a week passed during the winter of 1972 when new, important information did not stream in from either side of the Atlantic. When we visited my parents in March, I was already able to give the whole story to Dad, in its main outlines, and he in turn was able to give a few additional details as we sat and discussed in the evenings. I shall always be grateful that I began intensive work on this project just when I did, that I was able to learn so much so quickly, and that I had this chance to discuss it all with him on those winter evenings. Less than two weeks after we returned from that trip he died, suddenly and peacefully, at home.

For a time it was not easy to go on without him to share with me the joys of discovery. But the search continued. In the summer of 1973 we were able to visit Djursdala, where we stayed with Gösta Karlsson, his wife, Marianne, and their six children. Gösta and I discussed long and avidly. We called on Nils and Maria Olsson and their son, Dan, at Bullebo. By now I knew that Nils was a relative and it was comforting to know that the old farm was still in the family. He was the first of my relatives on the Svensson side I would meet in Sweden from that time on. We explored the old house, the barns and storehouses, the fields, and the shore of Lake Juttern. We saw Djursdala's seventeenth-century wooden church high on its hill, with its blackening shingled roof and walls, its peasant-baroque wall paintings of biblical scenes, its separate wooden bell tower, and the sweeping view from its churchyard wall over Djursdala village, Bullebo and its neighboring farms, and the lake, Juttern, extending, long and narrow, between forested hills and headlands, far to the north. In the neighboring parish of Södra Vi we found what I had hoped and expected I might eventually find. The Scandinavians take their family and local research seriously—as they have since the saga age—and with luck one's investigations may eventually lead to some previously unknown relative who has been exploring the same ground. At the Vidala old people's home in Södra Vi, Gösta took me to see my aging kinsman, Gunnar Olsson, formerly master of Kåreda farm. He could say little; his mind was beclouded by hardening of the arteries. But during the earlier 1960s he had, together with another mutual relative whom I had also known nothing about, prepared a family tree and history going all the way back into the later seventeenth century. His wife Kerstin brought out these documents and explained them while I took notes furiously. I would not see Gunnar Olsson again. He died early in 1975. Kerstin would be our invaluable cicerone when we explored the byways of Södra Vi and Djursdala parishes in search of the various ancestral farms during our next visit to the area, in August 1975.

The visit to Gunnar and Kerstin Olsson at the Vidala home in 1973 meanwhile put us in touch with another avid family historian, Gunnar's collaborator, Karin Augustinson, a brisk and active retired schoolteacher and church organist in her eighties. We did not then have the time to seek her out at her home in Ödeshög, in Östergötland near the northern end of Lake Vättern. But upon returning home that fall I wrote to her, thereby beginning a voluminous and immensely rewarding correspondence. She was as delighted to discover me as I was to find her, since she knew the history of the Swedish part of the family in great detail, following years of painstaking research and collecting of documents, but had long wondered what had become of the American branch: Sven Svensson, his eleven children, and all their descendants. I in turn already knew much about the Svenssons but was only beginning to learn something about those who had stayed home in Sweden.

Since the fall of 1973 Karin has been my invaluable collaborator. She has generously provided me with copies of many documents from her collection, including the estate inventories (*bouppteckningar*) for several of our ancestors going well back into the eighteenth century. She has dug out a great deal of additional information, much of it from the Vadstena provincial archive with the help of her former pupil Elsa Östblom of Vadstena. Not least of all I have grown greatly in my understanding of life in the old rural Sweden from the insightful commentaries in Karin's letters. She has to an admirable degree that kind of historical imagination that can transform the bare facts of old documents into a vivid, living picture of the past. During the summer of 1974 and on later trips to Sweden, we were able to visit her in Ödeshög.

Meanwhile, following our return from Sweden in 1973, we made another excursion, this time to Gowrie and certain other places in Iowa and northwestern Illinois connected with the family's history. Clifford Swenson was now nearing retirement age and his sons, Dean and James, who live nearby, were married and had children of their own. Their daughter, La Ceta Jane, also married, lives in Alaska, but the year before she had visited Djursdala and the Karlssons on the strength of information I had provided. Clifford was full of stories and recollections. We saw Grandfather Ernest's old "penny-farthing" bicycle, still in excellent condition, out in the barn. We visited the graves of Sven and Maria Svenson and several of their children and grandchildren in the Lost Grove Cemetery on its hill, on what was once Sven Svenson's land. We also visited Marie Anderson, still alone in her house on the old Svenson place, ailing but sharp of mind and memory; for a good two hours she answered my questions in surprising detail and right to the point, as fast as I could scribble notes on what she told me. When we left Gowrie, Clifford gave me a stack of family letters, in addition to those he had sent me earlier.

If I have dwelt lovingly upon the details of my search, it is because for a historian like myself the hunt itself is as exciting as the quarry, as will continue to be apparent in what follows. But the time has come to ask what results my search has led me to.

2

All the Way Back to Noah

Where should I begin? In Småland. The derivation of the name itself already tells us much. It means "small lands." The province occupies most of Sweden's so-called Southern Uplands; in contrast to the larger tribal kingdoms in the more fertile plains both to the north and south during the Bronze and early Iron Ages, population in this wilder terrain was sparse and widely scattered in small settlements where pockets of reasonably fertile soil could be found. Separating them were vast tracts of forest and heath, where the ground was too rocky, or in places, too sandy and gravelly to cultivate. The Swedish novelist Vilhelm Moberg, the great chronicler of the early emigration to America from those parts and himself a native of the province, has called it *"Stenriket"*—"the Stone Kingdom." [1] There is rock at every hand: in weathered granite outcroppings, in mossy boulders great and small scattered about the forest floor, in the tumbled debris of Ice Age moraines, in the massive rock piles in the fields and the grey stone walls around them that give mute testimony to the struggle of untold generations to wrest a living from the soil. There is a myriad of lakes of every size and configuration, and the ragged Baltic coast to the east breaks up into a maze of inlets, promontories, and islands.

If it is a hard land, it is also a beautiful one, ever dear to its wandering sons and daughters, whether they be in Stockholm or on the Iowa prairie. The northeastern corner, about which I am writing here, between the province of Östergötland and the Baltic, is especially lovely, at times almost heartrendingly so.

This is not simply my own, admittedly prejudiced view, for the Swedish government has recently designated the area around Djursdala as a specially protected environment because of its natural beauty. This is a steeper and hillier area than most of Småland.

I shall not forget how in 1971 I drove through it on a golden August day on the way from Stockholm to Copenhagen with my good friend, the Danish art historian Jørgen Schou-Christensen. As we came closer and closer to Djursdala (where we did not stop on this trip) I fell into a state of sweet yet melancholy reverie under the powerful spell of the passing landscape. How could my forebears have left all of this for the windswept prairie frontier out in Iowa? At the same time, reflecting on the great world beyond, I felt torn, as the American immigration historian Marcus Lee Hansen had when he had visited his ancestral island of Langeland in Denmark, between compassion for those "who were obliged to spend their lives year after year and generation after generation in the peace and quiet" of their ancient milieu, and at the same time for "their descendants who had been thrown into the fever and bustle and often fruitless activity of America." [2] Jørgen noticed my preoccupied silence and read my thoughts. "Yes," he said, "it is very beautiful to us. But do we really understand how it looked to them?"

That was it, exactly! I would later find a passage in the reminiscences which an elderly emigrant from the region immediately to the north, in Östergötland, wrote of his family's emigration for the *Fort Dodge Messenger* in Iowa (close to Gowrie) in 1880: "And now the old home is left forever, a home rough and rugged to be sure, but still a house where our cradles have stood, and where our pleasantest days of childhood have been passed, a place which to us children seemed a very paradise, but in our parents' eyes a place of misery and want to us after their efforts to secure a meager subsistence for their offspring should cease. But how many tender associations of our childhood we had to depart from. Often yet in my dreams I am carried back to that place." [3]

Beauty is in the eye of the beholder. My grandfather, Ernest, might yearn, at a sentimental moment in his later years, "to spend one whole Midsummer Day such as we had in Bullebo, with the halls decorated with greens and flowers, with the largest lilac hedge I ever saw in full bloom, and flaming peonies, and the lawn cropped close; then we would sit in the berceau and drink *hallonsaft* [raspberry juice] and be happy."[4] He had left the old home forever at the age of nine. Yet who is to say that true beauty for his father, Sven Svenson, after his years of toil and disappointment at Bullebo, was not to be found in his broad acres of stone-free Iowa plowland? "I never knew a man that loved the soil as did Father," Ernest wrote of him. "Mind you, it was not for what it would bring; he just loved it for its own sake. When he looked over a field of rich, dark loam then he closed his lips tight in satisfaction."[5] I have seen the same expression on my own father's face—though he never saw his grandfather Sven—in moments of deep contentment. Dad remembered hearing that Sven loved to go outside on warm summer evenings in Iowa and "just listen to the corn grow."

The people of Småland—the *smålänningar*—have been shaped by their austere yet lovely surroundings. Among Swedes they have a reputation for being practical, frugal, hardworking, and resourceful. Put a *smålänning* and a goat on a rocky islet somewhere, the saying goes, and they will somehow find a way to get along. Or even prosper, as numerous shrewd *smålänningar* have managed to do throughout Sweden, North America, and more remote corners of the world—and even in Småland itself! They are known as a proud and independent people, patient yet stubborn. At the same time they are held to possess a dreamy and poetic strain that has found expression in Swedish—and in some cases even American—art and literature. All of these traits are to be found in the clan that concerns us here.

We may next ask ourselves at what point in time we ought to begin our account. "About Father," Ernest once wrote, "his ancestors were farmers all the way back to Noah."[6] Surely they had tilled the rocky soil of their corner of Småland since time immemorial. If we cannot trace them back that far, we nonetheless find the first fully verifiable forebear emerging from the mists of the mid-seventeenth century. We know that he was called Carl and that he lived at Loxbo in Södra Vi parish.

The name Loxbo is believed to have derived from something like "the peasant Lock's *fäbod*," which means a simple shelter on a remote summer pasture.[7] Loxbo is on the edge of rough, broken terrain, with steep hillside patches of stony field and pasture hard against the brow of the forest, but also includes good arable land on what must be the bed of a prehistoric lake. We can thus imagine that at some early time of population growth, most likely in the sixteenth century, one of "Lock's" descendants, a younger son in a numerous family, moved out from the cultivated core of the old village by Lake Krön—whose name, Södra Vi, "the southern cult place," bespeaks its origins in pre-Christian times—to clear and settle on his family's summer pasture, not unlike his own later descendants, who in time would clear and settle lands in a new wilderness across the western sea.

The earliest recorded occupant at Loxbo indeed dates back to the reign of King Gustav Vasa in the mid-sixteenth century. He was called "Per at Loxbo" and is mentioned in the tax rolls for 1538 as a *skattebonde*, or independent peasant landowner.[8]

The use of the term "peasant" as a translation for the Swedish *bonde* requires some qualification. My grandfather, Ernest, chose to describe his ancestors, back to Noah's time, as "farmers" in English, the term my father likewise insisted on using, for the Swedish *bönder*—unlike the oppressed peasantry of most of Europe—had always been free men and were intensely proud of that fact. In most periods the majority of them were also *skattebönder*, owning their own farms in full title, and were thus represented by their own fourth estate in the Swedish *riksdag*, or diet, a situation unparalleled anywhere else outside of Scandinavia.

It was as free subjects of their king that the Swedish peasantry bore its heavy share of the burdens of state. From their perspective, their country's history during the wars and conquests of the sixteenth and seventeenth centuries was the story of constant, pressing taxes, which fortunately for the historian were conscientiously recorded by the responsible authorities. It has been through the records of, among other things, taxes in grain, butter, and specie, of royal mill fees and labor service for transport and road maintenance, of special levies for the ransoming of captured fortresses, and of recruitment of men for the army, preserved in the provincial and national archives, that Karin Augustinson was gradually able to account for Carl's predecessors at Loxbo all the way back to 1538.

It was not an easy search: "How many times [she wrote to me at one point] have I not seen our progenitor, Per at Loxbo, wandering tantalizingly among his low, turf-roofed, log farm buildings, tending to his own and his family's affairs! He has appeared, furtive and mysterious, more like the misty figure of fantasy than a tangible human being, always slipping away and disappearing behind the house-corner in the most frustrating way."[9]

Yet with time Per has been adequately documented. The tithe records mention him again in 1558 and indicate that he was at Loxbo until 1569. In the later 1560s, during the Seven Years' War of the North, a Danish force commanded by Daniel Rantzau passed through the area. According to local tradition, the inhabitants of Loxbo withdrew into the woods, where they created such a racket by firing their harquebuses and banging on iron pots that the Danes were tricked into believing they were an approaching Swedish army and hastily withdrew.[10]

Per was followed in 1570 by Lasse at Loxbo, who contributed to the first ransom of Älvsborg fortress from the Danes following the war in 1571. He in turn was succeeded by Nils, from 1579 to 1591, followed by Jon, who is, however, first mentioned in 1598, was taxed for Älvsborg's second ransom from the Danes in 1613–18, and had the responsible position of *nämndeman*, or permanent juryman, which would indicate that he was a man of some standing in the parish. Jon was followed in 1624 by his son, Måns Jonsson, who likewise served as a *nämndeman* from 1623 and in 1628–29 is listed among the soldiers (*krigsfolk*) for the locality. It was at this very time, in 1628, that King Gustav II

Adolf, following a series of wars against the Danes, Poles, and Muscovites, began his fateful intervention in the Thirty Years' War in the Holy Roman Empire and we can well imagine that Måns and his companions marched off to campaign across the Baltic. It is not unlikely, too, that he failed to return, for in 1635, and again in 1647, the tax rolls show that Carl was now the farmer at Loxbo, to be followed in 1671 by his son, Arvid.[11]

Before Carl in 1635 it is not clear what the relationship between these persons may have been, except that Jon and Måns were father and son. It is quite probable that they represent six generations of the same family. The names Per, Nils, Jon, and Måns would all recur among Arvid's children and grandchildren. We cannot, however, exclude the possibility that the farm might have passed at one point or another to a cousin, nephew, son-in-law, or even to another family between 1538 and 1635.

Karin Augustinson has written that Per at Loxbo in the sixteenth century "is like a boundary stone between the known and the unknown."[12] Similarly, Carl stands, a century later, at the head of our verifiable family tree, with its branches extending to the present day. About him we know next to nothing, except that he was the father of Arvid Carlsson. Of Carl's grandson, Oluf Arvidsson, the preserved records give a somewhat fuller picture. When I wrote to Karin Augustinson in late 1975 that I finally intended to start writing this family history, she had not yet traced the occupants of Loxbo before Oluf in 1681. She therefore replied:

> I would begin . . . on a weekday in the 1680s at Loxbo, when Oluf arises early. I know exactly how he is dressed through the estate inventories—a couple of generations inherited each other's clothing. I know the names of the cows he would milk and what they looked like. We know what other animals he had to feed before hitching his only horse to the ancient wooden plow [*årder*], which could not turn the soil but only scratch a furrow in it. The goodwife in the kitchen, the appearance of which we also know, is in her gray and threadbare everyday garb. She cooks her porridge on the open fire and sets the primitive wooden table with spoons

and plates of wood—and so forth and so on. One could go on endlessly, thanks to the rich materials which the estate inventories permit us to draw upon.[13]

Indeed we could continue at great length, given the remarkably full and complete records of births, marriages, deaths, domiciles, property transfers, taxation, church attendance, literacy, and similar matters maintained in Sweden from the early eighteenth century. They are indeed unsurpassed anywhere. I give this excerpt from Karin's letter to show how effectively such material can be used to reconstruct the past. And no one can do so with greater sensitivity and insight than she.

We also know, from later studies, much of the social and psychological world in which Oluf and the generations that followed him lived out their lives: the traditions that governed the planting and the harvesting, birth, marriage, and death, Christmas and Midsummer; the folk wisdom conveyed from generation to generation—like the goods and chattels of ancient farms —through countless proverbs, sayings, and songs, prescribing behavior for all the recurrent situations of a changeless way of life; the natural remedies for the ailments afflicting man and beast; the sturdy piety in the Lutheran faith of their fathers combined with ageless beliefs that went back far before the coming of the White Christ to the North; the "other world" of good household elves and malignant forest trolls, of the spirits of lake, river, and woodland, of the ghosts of the dead who returned to their old farmsteads on Christmas Eve.[14]

Thus although we cannot summon the face and form of old Oluf before our mind's eye, we can know much about how he lived and what he thought and felt. People, particularly the peasantry, were smaller in those days and we may picture Oluf as short of stature but tough, wiry, and weather-beaten. We do not know how many children he had, but when he died in 1723 he was followed at Loxbo by his son, Stephan (or Staffan) Olufsson, born in 1683.

Stephan's estate inventory, dated 17 February 1748, following his death, shows him to have occupied "1/3 del skatte frälse" at

1. The farmers at Loxbo, Södra Vi, 1538–1671

Per at Loxbo	1538–69
Lasse	1570–79
Nils	1579–91
Jon	1598–1624
Måns Jonsson	1624–? (son of Jon)
Carl	1635–71

[See chart 2]

NOTE: Dates refer to occupancy of the farm.

2. Carl at Loxbo and his descendants, 1635–1858

Carl (at Loxbo, 1635–71)
|
Arvid Carlsson (at Loxbo, 1671–81)
|
Oluf Arvidsson (farmer at Loxbo, 1681; died 1723)
|
Stephan Olufsson (lived 1683–1748)

    Married 3 times; 9 children

    Second wife: Annica Isaksdotter (1681–1745)
|
Arvid Steffansson (lived 1731–1806)

    Married to Karin Jonsdotter (1743–1809)

    3 children
|
Sven Arvidsson (lived 1781–1858)

    Married to Maja Nilsdotter (1786–1853)

    6 children

[See chart 3]

3. The Arvidsson-Öhrn-Svensson family, 1781–1908

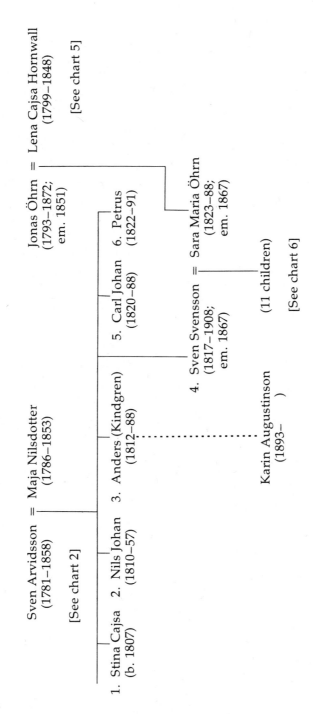

NOTE: Broken line indicates descent without showing intervening generations.

Loxbo, which requires some explanation. This amounted to one-third of a *mantal*, which was a fiscal unit, not a fixed unit of measurement. Since the 1630s the government had assessed landholdings into *mantal* or "full homesteads": farms adjudged large and productive enough to provide a reasonable living to the occupant and his household, plus a certain yearly land tax to the state. The size of a *mantal* thus varied considerably from one part of the country to another, depending upon the extent and quality of arable land and other productive resources; in poor, stony Småland a *mantal* was usually quite large in area, including a good deal of forest and rough pasture.

Carl at Loxbo is shown in the tax rolls for 1635 as the holder of a full *mantal*.[15] As the government at first prohibited the division of *mantal* holdings, we may envision Loxbo farmstead in his and his immediate successors' time as a sizable cluster of dwellings and outbuildings, inhabited by numerous relatives and retainers. During the eighteenth century the recognized *mantal* size for each farm became stabilized. The government now permitted the splitting of *mantal* holdings into half, or at the most, quarter allotments. In actual practice, however, population pressure on the land led among the peasantry to the acquisition of odd and increasingly smaller fractions of *mantal* properties. Thus Stephan Olufsson's one-third of a *mantal* consisted in turn of two one-sixth shares, acquired separately in 1711 and 1719. By his time Loxbo had evolved into a little hamlet. Parenthetically, it might be added that the old *mantal* assessment disappeared after 1892 with the elimination of the ancient land tax system it served.

Carl's land at Loxbo is designated in 1635 as *skatte frälse*, as is Stephan's in his purchase contracts of 1711 and 1719, and his estate inventory of 1748. This, too, tells something of the changes that had taken place in the Swedish countryside since the sixteenth century. Per at Loxbo is listed on the tax rolls for 1538 as a *skattebonde*, or peasant proprietor. During the seventeenth century, however, under the financial pressures of their European wars, Sweden's monarchs donated, in return for services or loans, or sold outright both crown estates and the tax revenues deriving from independent peasant freeholds to members of the nobility. In the latter case, the peasant remained proprietor of his land—now designated as a *skatte frälse* holding— but paid his tax to the noble purchaser of the taxation privilege. This is evidently what happened to Loxbo, sometime prior to 1635. Such alienations of crown lands and revenues assumed ruinous proportions by the mid-seventeenth century—the golden age of Sweden's aristocracy—and the peasant owners of *skatte frälse* farms had to struggle to defend their old status as freeholders and to avoid being reduced to that of tenants on noble manorial estates. In the 1680s Charles XI reappropriated the royal donations, although not the sold rights and properties, through the so-called *reduktion* and reasserted the rights of peasant proprietors, including the owners of *skatte frälse* land.[16]

We can only speculate over the tribulations these developments may have brought for the masters of Loxbo during the era of aristocratic predominance. But thereafter their prospects brightened. The Great Northern War (1700–1721), during which Sweden's warrior king, Charles XII, fought his way throughout eastern Europe against a host of enemies, was, like many wars, a time of opportunity for many enterprising cultivators of the soil, as were the decades of peace and rising prosperity which followed. Stephan Olufsson was apparently one of them. His estate inventory in 1748 shows land evaluated at 200 *daler* in silver, plus 153 *daler* in cash, a good wardrobe, a sizable stock of tools, implements, and utensils of all kinds, a herd of forty-seven animals, and even a few objects in silver—four ornamented goblets, one gilded, and two spoons. His total worth is reckoned at 662 *daler*, 9 *skilling*, in silver. Of this inventory, Karin Augustinson has written:

> When I sit and read it, I wish that the estate evaluators had depicted the people on the farm as graphically as the horses, oxen, cows, heifers, bull calves, sheep, and pigs are described in detail. Stephan lived in a large chamber, with various "hangings and covers" for "the north bed, the east bed, the south bed." From the carefully itemized garments we know exactly how he was dressed, and on solemn occasions he car-

ried a "cane with a brass knob." . . . Fifteen scythes were at work during the haymaking; fifteen sickles could clean up after them. Doesn't it sound wonderful!

This inheritance had, meanwhile, to be divided many ways, which led to contention and eventually to court proceedings among the heirs.[17] This would unfortunately not be the last time that Stephan's descendants would quarrel and even go to court over inheritances. Stephan had been married three times and had sired nine children, only one of whom, strange to say for that time, seems to have died in infancy. It was not uncommon, however, for a man to outlive several wives—as we shall see more than once—before medical advances in the later nineteenth century would reduce the fearsome risks of childbirth. The sixth of Stephan's eight offspring by his second wife, Annica Isaksdotter, was Arvid Steffansson, born in 1731, who remained at Loxbo.

Once again, the estate inventory drawn up following the death of Arvid Steffansson in 1806 tells us most of what we are able to learn about him. He left behind him 15/24 of a *mantal*; of this he had inherited one-sixth of a *mantal*, the rest he acquired through purchase, partly from his co-heirs, and through marriage. Although his total worth is given as 1,081:18 *riksdaler specie*, we may not automatically conclude that he died better off than his father because of intervening currency changes and the widely fluctuating value of money during his lifetime. The listing of his goods and chattels is in most respects less impressive than Stephan Olufsson's in 1748; he left, for instance, only two cows, a sow, and a sheep. Yet he had managed to accumulate more land than his father had held and he died free of debt. No less important for the following generation, he was married only once, to Karin Jonsdotter, who bore him only three children, two sons and a daughter.

This circumstance was surely of considerable importance for Arvid's second son, Sven Arvidsson, born in 1781, since it gave him a sufficient start in life to make him an eligible suitor for the hand of Maja Nilsdotter, the heiress to the prosperous master of Halsjöbo farm, whom he married in 1806, shortly before his father's death. Sven Arvidsson would become something of a legend in his own time. His marriage brought him wealth and social standing. Throughout his life he bought and sold land in Södra Vi and nearby parishes and engaged in lengthy property suits against various of his neighbors.

My grandfather, Ernest, spoke proudly of him: "Father's father left a big, fine farm for each of his seven children." This was not too far from the truth: Sven Arvidsson had six children who actually reached maturity and he provided well for all of them, indeed giving four of his sons farms of their own. For himself he bought Karsnäs farm on the fertile land by Lake Krön, close to Södra Vi church-village, the center of the parish. This farm eventually went to his oldest son, Nils Johan. The second son, Anders, who took the name Kindgren and from whom Karin Augustinson is descended, became master of the old Rumskulla Manor in neighboring Rumskulla parish; the third and fourth sons, Sven—my great-grandfather—and Carl Johan, a farmer and innkeeper in Horn, Östergötland, were given equal shares of Bullebo farm in Djursdala parish; the fifth son, Petrus, obtained the lease of Kåreda farm in Södra Vi parish from a sister-in-law. We may assume that Sven Arvidsson's oldest child and only daughter, Stina Cajsa, who moved to Frödinge parish after great traditional wedding festivities at Karsnäs in 1825, received a generous dowry. It was said of Sven Arvidsson that he could walk through three adjoining parishes—Rumskulla, Södra Vi, and Djursdala—on his own land.[18] It was of him and his family that Gösta Karlsson was able in 1972 to pass on to me the old rhyme, still remembered in the area: "Att heta von i andra länder/ Är lika fint som Svensson vid Kröns stränder" (approximately: "A name with *von* in other lands/ Is as fine as Svensson by Lake Krön's strand.")[19]

The estate inventories of Maja Nilsdotter after her death in 1854 and of Sven Arvidsson in 1858 seem more modest than we might expect until we take into account how much of their wealth and property they had already passed on to their children. The numerous credits and debits itemized in their inventories meanwhile show how actively engaged they remained to the end in a variety of financial transactions. Maja Nilsdotter left assets estimated at 5,819:35 *riksdaler* in silver and Sven Arvidsson of 7,991:95 *riksdaler*.

Two circumstances deserve at this point more than our passing notice. First, much if not most of the landed property Sven Arvidsson bought for himself and his children was *frälsejord* or manorial land, outright ownership of which was formerly the exclusive privilege of the nobility. Gustav III removed this legal restriction for outlying manorial lands in 1789; in 1809 all remaining *frälsejord* was made freely purchasable. The principal beneficiaries were the peasantry, who throughout the nineteenth century acquired in clear title increasing amounts of formerly noble domain.[20] Secondly, Sven Arvidsson was literate, able not only to read but to write as well. I have the lease for a *torp*, or croft, on his land from 1843, in his hand. All of the heirs and witnesses present for his wife's estate inventory in 1854 and his own in 1858 signed their own names, even though Sweden did not establish a regular, compulsory system of elementary education before the School Law of 1842, which was only slowly put into effect throughout the country. The heirs and witnesses at Stephan Olufsson's estate inventory in 1748 had only been able to sign with their *bomärken*—the sign representing each farmstead, similar to the brand in the American West—or at best with their initials. Those who signed Arvid Steffansson's estate inventory in 1806 had meanwhile been able to write their whole names, even though the handwriting is crude.[21] Together these circumstances give mute evidence of the steady rise of the Swedish peasantry in status, prosperity, and enlightenment since the beginning of the eighteenth century.

In his later years Sven Arvidsson could take satisfaction in his children, who had married respectably and advantageously, and diligently cultivated farms of their own. All, that is, except the youngest son. Of him, Kerstin Olsson wrote to me: "Petrus Svensson's economy was not so good. He lived too high. When he was working the North Farm at Kåreda, which was owned by his sister-in-law, Sara Vändla at Venefall, he had two fine coach horses, fine harness with nickel-plated accoutrements, and a fine carriage. He often drove into town, so that work on the farm fell behind."²² After only five years at Kåreda he left and thereafter drifted from one place to another until he died in 1891, leaving considerable debts to numerous persons, inside and outside of his family. Petrus too, with his restless and improvident nature, tells us something of his times. Fresh winds were blowing through the Swedish countryside, stirring new dreams, ambitions, and pretensions. In Petrus we seem to sense already the later destinies of certain of his brother Sven's children across the ocean in the New World.

It is time that we turned our attention to Sven. He was born at Karsnäs farm in Södra Vi on 23 March 1817, the fifth child of Sven Arvidsson and Maja Nilsdotter. His immediate predecessor, a boy born in 1815 who died already the following year, had also been named Sven. According to an ancient custom the next child in the family, being of the same sex, was given the same name in the belief that it possessed the returned soul of the deceased infant. This second Sven would reach the age of ninety-one years, surviving all of his family. We know little of his childhood years at Karsnäs except that he evidently received a good schooling for the rural Sweden of his time. The letters I presently possess by him, from the year 1876, are written in a fine copper-plate hand, a notable improvement over his father's. From his early years he surely had his share of farmyard chores to do and learned the varied tasks of the farmer's calendar. In 1841 he showed up at the farm at Smitterstad in Odensvi parish, between Södra Vi and the Baltic, owned by Jonas Larsson Öhrn, whose daughter, Sara Maria, Sven married in Odensvi church on 30 May that same year.

The day before, on 29 May 1841, Gustaf Unonius, a government clerk from Uppsala, embarked from Gävle for the United States, together with his young wife, their maid, and two university students. He would thereafter call himself Sweden's "first emigrant," since he was the first to leave under a new law allowing emigration without the king's special permission. He was hardly that, however, for occasional Swedes had been finding their way to the New World since colonial times. The departure of the Unonius party and the establishment of their little colony of "New Uppsala" at Pine Lake, Wisconsin, nonetheless attracted much attention in Sweden, especially through the publication of Gustaf Unonius's letters home in the Stockholm newspaper, *Aftonbladet*, in 1842.[23] Their venture has thus come to be traditionally regarded as the real beginning of the great Swedish migration across the sea, although a quarter century would still elapse before it would reach very substantial proportions.

It seems doubtful that the newly married couple at Smitterstad in Odensvi parish—far from Stockholm and Uppsala—knew anything of this at the time. And even if they did, they would scarcely have imagined that it could possibly have anything whatsoever to do with their own future.

3

First Link
with the New World

Throughout the great migration, a large majority of those who crossed the Atlantic went to join relatives and friends from home already established in North America. They, in turn, drew others after them in ever-widening chain reactions. The more Swedes there came to be in the new land, the more familiar it became to those they had left behind. Yet each of these largely self-generating chain reactions had to begin somewhere: with an individual who as yet knew no one who had ever been in America, but still was prepared to make a great leap of faith into a new world and a new life only dimly perceived.

Dad always believed that the first link in the chain of emigrants that came to include Sven Svensson and his numerous family was "Old Öhrn," who had come to America "very early," as we have noted. I naturally assumed the same, and went to great pains in 1972–75 to uncover his tracks, as will be recounted in the following chapter. Only in the eleventh hour—when the manuscript of this book was already under consideration by the publisher—did Karin Augustinson happen to discover in the Vadstena provincial archive the family's actual first link with the New World among the founders of the first lasting Swedish settlement in the American Midwest.[1]

His name was Peter Andersson and he was born on the croft, Lilla Brohult, in Tryserum parish in northeasternmost Småland, near the shore of the Baltic, in 1817—the same year as Sven Svensson. He was the third of the five children of a poor crofter (*torpare*), Anders Jaensson, and his wife, Lena Hindricsdotter. Anders died of consumption already in 1822, in his forty-sixth year, leaving his pregnant wife and four children destitute. By 1825 Lena Hindricsdotter disappears from the Tryserum parish records and her family became dispersed. Peter, then eight, was placed that year in the home of a farmer in nearby Östra Ed parish. Although his two brothers later turned up in the same parish and one sister in Västervik, it is unclear what at first became of them. It is possible that the children were farmed out to relatives, but one may also wonder whether they might not have become wards of various parishes and been "auctioned" off to whichever local families bid lowest to the parish poor funds for their support, according to a system which survived in rural Sweden into the early years of this century.

Already in 1827 Peter moved to a fisherman's family in the same parish, in 1829 to a family in Västra Ed parish, in 1833 to a crofter in Lofta parish, in 1834 to a blacksmith back in Västra Ed, who moved in 1835 with his family and Peter to Kläckeberga parish, some distance to the south, near Kalmar. In November 1839 Baron Victor Fleetwood came from Kläckeberga to Odensvi parish to take charge of Ogestad manor, bringing with him four farm laborers, of whom Peter Andersson, now twenty-two, became a foreman (*rättare*).[2]

Two years later, in October 1841—less than five months after Sven Svensson had wed Sara Maria Öhrn in the same church—Peter married Christina Lovisa Fagerström, born in 1818 on Ogestad manor, where her father was also a foreman. The Fagerströms were a respected local family, and the marriage shows that the poor boy from Tryserum was coming up in the world. In July 1842 Christina bore a daughter, Sophia Christina, and in August 1844, a son, Anders August.

On 12 April 1845 the records of the county (*län*) administration in Kalmar show that Farm Foreman Peter Andersson took out a passport for "North America," for himself and his family.[3] What could have caused him to make so unprecedented a move? What could a twenty-eight-year-old farm worker with doubtless no more than the most rudimentary schooling, in a district from which no immigration to America had yet taken place, know of the Great Land in the West? We have already noted the emigration in May 1841 of Gustaf Unonius and four other persons from Uppsala, who established themselves at Pine Lake, Wisconsin. Unonius's letters from the little settlement, published in the liberal Stockholm newspaper, *Aftonbladet*, aroused considerable interest in educated circles, leading to the immigration of several upper-class persons to the Pine Lake colony, either for idealistic reasons or because of personal difficulties at home. As they lacked the practical skills necessary for frontier farming, the settlement broke up after only a few years; Unonius himself became an Episcopalian priest and moved to Chicago, where a number of the other Pine Lake settlers also ended up. In the meantime, however, the appeal of Pine Lake had spread to new quarters.

In 1842, Polycarpus von Schneidau, a young officer of the elite Svea Artillery Regiment in Stockholm who had committed the indiscretion of marrying a Jewess, immigrated with his young wife to Pine Lake. His letters to his father in Kisa parish in southern Östergötland attracted much attention locally and were read by, among others, Peter (Pehr) Cassel at Bjerkeryd, a respected miller and housebuilder. Cassel's earlier activities reveal his growing discontent with conditions in Sweden. In 1844 he had signed a petition calling for the representational reform of the *Riksdag* or parliament, then still consisting of the four medieval Estates of the Nobility, Clergy, Burghers, and landowning Peasants, which gained him a reputation for liberal political views. He had also been active in pietistic and temperance circles. In *Aftonbladet* he had read both Unonius's account and that of the prominent Norwegian emigrant, Hans Gasmann, who in 1843 led a group of his countrymen to Pine Lake. He had even learned some English. Now at the age of fifty-four, Peter Cassel set about organizing a group of his own kinsmen in Kisa parish to emigrate to America. Early in May 1845 three families and two single persons, a group of seventeen Kisa residents, took out passports in Linköping for North America, causing some sensation in the newspapers. A "Traveler in

Östergötland" reported meeting some of the emigrants in Kisa before their departure in an article in *Najaden* (Karlskrona) which was later reprinted in *Aftonbladet* (Stockholm); he described Peter Cassel as a peasant "genius," deplored conditions which caused such relatively well-to-do farmers to depart, pointed out that they comprised "the first emigrant group of any size from our country," and predicted that "hundreds" of other Swedes would surely follow them.[4]

Traveling by wagon and canal boat, the Cassel party arrived in Gothenburg on 21 May and found that the ship on which they had booked passage had been declared unseaworthy. They thus arranged to sail on the bark *Superb*, which was to depart for New York the following month. In the meantime, its captain, J. E. Nissen, let them stay on his farm outside the city, where the men worked on the construction of his new house in return for lodging.

It would be easy to imagine that Peter Andersson and his family from Odensvi were a part of the Cassel group from the start, and indeed this has been assumed without question by earlier historians.[5] Yet a closer investigation brings to light no family or other personal ties between the Anderssons and any members of the Cassel party from Kisa, all of whom were related to each other by blood or marriage. Neither Peter nor Christina Andersson had ever lived in the province of Östergötland. Moreover they had taken out their passport for North America in Kalmar already on 12 April, before Cassel and his group received permits to emigrate in Kisa between 17 and 24 April, and their passports in Linköping on 3 May.[6]

Thus, while some indirect influence from the Cassel group and even the Pine Lake settlement cannot be altogether ruled out, it is evident that Peter Andersson—like Karl-Oskar Nilsson, the hero of Vilhelm Moberg's classic novel, *The Emigrants*—had to reach his decision to emigrate on his own, and surely in the face of great skepticism and even hostility in his home community. He thus strikingly exemplifies a new spirit that was then beginning to make itself felt in the Swedish countryside, which refused to accept existing conditions simply because they had always been that way, or even because God in His infinite wisdom had so ordained. One may speculate whether Peter, who held a responsible position on a large landed estate, may not have been especially exposed to new and progressive ideas. The proprietor since 1777 of the much larger Odensviholm manor, Johan Fredrik Granschoug, who died in 1839, was long remembered for his ambitious and innovative spirit, which may also have left some mark on the inhabitants of Odensvi, in contrast to surrounding parishes.[7]

Be that as it may, Peter's and Christina's decision could only have been a hard and lonely one. Their son was less than a year old, their daughter not yet three. Yet what kind of a future awaited the family in rural Sweden, without land of their own? About America they can only have had the vaguest of conceptions. No other emigrants joined them from their home parish. As they left Odensvi, they faced the future alone, until they fell in with Peter Cassel's group from Kisa, which they evidently did after reaching Gothenburg.

Two others meanwhile joined the group: A. C. Berg, a shoemaker from Stockholm, and Otto Vilhelm Åkerman, a bookkeeper who had first gone to America in 1840 and had served four years in the U.S. Army before returning to Sweden in 1844. On 24 June the *Superb* at last departed Gothenburg.[8]

It would be a long time still before there would be any regular, scheduled sailings from Sweden to the United States. A number of sailing vessels, such as the *Superb*, did however make the crossing at irregular intervals, carrying Swedish bar-iron to American ports, as well as such travelers as sought passage. These were packed into the between decks as an additional cargo on top of the iron, except for those few who could pay for more comfortable quarters. The *Superb*'s passenger list upon arrival in New York counts thirty-eight persons, most of them members of Cassel's growing party. They were fortunate that their sea voyage took no more than eight weeks, for with heavy weather and contrary winds the westerly passage could easily have been prolonged to three, or even four months on the heaving ocean. The *Superb*'s crossing during the height of the summer of 1845 seems to have been relatively uneventful for the sailing ship era, although one of Peter Cassel's sons later recalled heavy storms in the English Channel and again in mid-ocean, leading to a collision with another vessel which cost the *Superb* her bowsprit.[9]

Despite numerous descriptions from that period, we can scarcely picture to ourselves the ordeal of emigrant ocean travel under sail: the moldy ship's biscuit and putrid water; the ever-damp and mildewing clothing and blankets; the crowding of the dimly lit emigrants' quarters; the spread of body lice; the suffocating stench, particularly when the hatches had to be battened down for days at a time during rough weather; the chilling winds and rain squalls on deck; the retching of the seasick and fearful cries of those delirious with shipboard fevers. While the Cassel group was fortunate not to lose any of its members at sea, shipboard deaths were frequent enough at the time and during spells of calmer weather those whose strength had proved unequal to the test were committed to the deep.[10] For most of those who made it to the further shore the memory of the Atlantic crossing stood like a wall barring any thought of ever returning to the land of their birth again.

The *Superb* reached New York on 11 August, anchoring near the Methodist floating chapel, the Bethel Ship *John Wesley*, aboard which the former Swedish seaman, Olof Hedström, had in May begun his Scandinavian mission. The Cassel party was among the first of the thousands of Swedish immigrants Hedström would welcome and assist upon their arrival in New York, down to his retirement in 1875. He may well have strongly impressed Peter Cassel and others of his group who had felt some dissatisfaction with religious conditions under the state church in Sweden and who would themselves later become Methodists. Most likely, too, Hedström urged the group to settle in western Illinois, where his brother, Jonas, was living in Victoria, Henry County; a few months later, in December 1845, Olof Hedström would persuade Olof Olsson, the advance scout for the Erik Janssonist sectaries from north-central Sweden, to seek land near Victoria, Illinois, for the Bishop Hill colony founded the following year.[11] Over the years Olof Hedström in New York would direct a growing stream of Swedish settlers to the prairies of western Illinois.

Cassel and the Kisa emigrants had originally intended to make their way to the Pine Lake settlement in Wisconsin. (Where Peter Andersson and his family had thought of going we have no way of knowing.) Various alternatives now presented themselves. In New York the group met a former Swedish sea captain, Peter (Pehr) Dahlberg, who had been in America since 1843 and had come to meet his wife and children on the *Carolina*, which arrived from Stockholm on the same day as the *Superb*. Dahlberg had spent some time at Pine Lake but considered the soil poor and advised against settling there. Otto Åkerman had meanwhile served at Fort Des Moines while in the U.S. Army, and together with Dahlberg and Berg persuaded the group to seek land in Iowa instead.[12]

After a few days in New York, the party, including the Dahlberg family—now thirty-two persons in all—continued their journey, by steamboat and railroad to Philadelphia, then by rail and horse-drawn canal boat to Pittsburgh. While crossing Pennsylvania the party lost its first member: Peter and Christina Andersson's little son, Anders August, who died of a fever close to his first birthday on a canal boat and had to be buried along the way. Soon after two little girls, one a daughter of Peter Cassel, died of typhoid fever.[13]

At Pittsburgh the party boarded a riverboat, which took them down the Ohio River to Cairo, Illinois, where they took another boat up the Mississippi. During a stop in St. Louis, it is recounted that they saw black slaves being sold at auction—surely a strange and sobering experience for peasants from the Swedish countryside. At last they arrived at Burlington, Iowa, then the territorial capital with some thirteen hundred inhabitants, in early September.[14]

At the government land office in Burlington it was found that the nearest public land available for settlement lay in Jefferson County, some 40 miles to the west. The men soon set off to scout the possibilities. A. C. Berg negotiated for the purchase of a tract from a man in Burlington, but when he and the other members of the group could not agree on the terms, Berg went his own way. Two "educated countrymen" from Västergötland now entered the picture and Peter Cassel wrote home on 9 February 1846 that together they were thinking of taking land on the Des Moines River, some 140 miles to the west. For unexplained reasons this plan fell through. By this time the group was living as squatters near Brush Creek, about four miles northwest of the present town of Lockridge in Jefferson County, and here they would remain to found their New Sweden settlement.[15] In Wisconsin, Gustaf Unonius's Pine Lake colony was by this time beginning to break up. New Sweden, Iowa, dating from the fall of 1845 thus remains the oldest lasting Swedish settlement in the American Midwest.

The families first sought shelter in a tumbledown shack left by an early pioneer, which they roofed over with bulrushes and named "New Stockholm." During the winter two or three of the families built themselves log huts. The men meanwhile took such employment in the area as they could find. Åkerman reenlisted in the army at Fort Des Moines and was killed three years later in a skirmish with the Indians in New Mexico.[16]

In the meantime, Peter Cassel's letter to his "friends and countrymen" in Kisa of 9 February 1846, mentioned above, contained a glowing account of conditions in the new land. "The ease of making a living here and the increasing prosperity of the farmers, year by year and day by day, exceeds anything we anticipated. If only half the work expended on the soil in the fatherland were utilized here, the yield would reach the wildest imagination." The surface of the ground, he added—surely with telling effect upon his friends in Kisa parish—contained "not a single stone," though there was limestone for building purposes at a depth of several feet, as well as coal along the creek-beds, and plenty of hardwood forest. Fish and game abounded. Everyone could have as much livestock as he wished, since "pasturage is common property, extending from one end of the land to the other. . . . All crops thrive and grow to an astonishing degree. Cornfields look more like woods than grain fields. . . .

4. The descendants of Olof and Sara Greta Fagerström, Odensvi

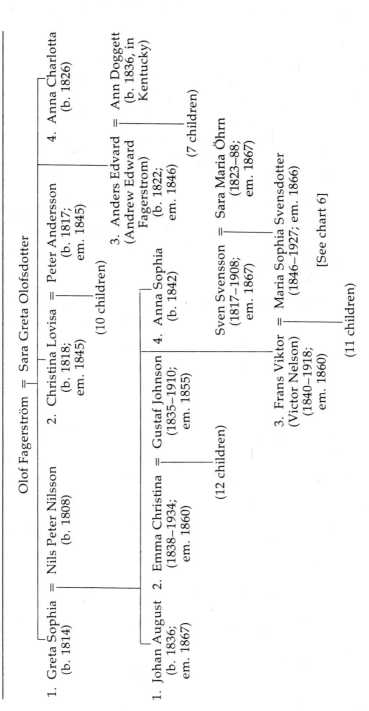

Olof Fagerström = Sara Greta Olofsdotter

1. Greta Sophia = Nils Peter Nilsson
(b. 1814)   (b. 1808)

2. Christina Lovisa = Peter Andersson
(b. 1818;   (b. 1817;
em. 1845)   em. 1845)

(10 children)

4. Anna Charlotta
(b. 1826)

3. Anders Edvard = Ann Doggett
(Andrew Edward   (b. 1836, in
Fagerstrom)   Kentucky)
(b. 1822;
em. 1846)

(7 children)

1. Johan August
(b. 1836;
em. 1867)

2. Emma Christina = Gustaf Johnson
(1838–1934;   (1835–1910;
em. 1860)   em. 1855)

(12 children)

4. Anna Sophia
(b. 1842)

Sven Svensson = Sara Maria Öhrn
(1817–1908;   (1823–88;
em. 1867)   em. 1867)

3. Frans Viktor = Maria Sophia Svensdotter
(Victor Nelson)   (1846–1927; em. 1866)
(1840–1918;
em. 1860)

[See chart 6]

(11 children)

A bushel of seed corn yields as high as seven hundred bushels." Wages were high and American food "unusually good." Turning from the material blessings of the new land, Cassel continued: "Freedom and equality are the fundamental principles of the Constitution of the United States. There is no such thing as class distinction here, no counts, barons, lords, or lordly estates. The one is as good as another, and everyone lives in the unrestricted enjoyment of personal liberty. A Swedish *bonde* [peasant], raised under oppression and accustomed to poverty and want, here finds himself elevated to a new world, as it were, where all his former hazy ideas of a society conforming more closely to nature's laws are suddenly made real and he enjoys a satisfaction in life that he has never before experienced. There are no beggars here and there never can be so long as the people are ruled by the spirit that prevails now."

The local population, Cassel wrote, consisted mainly of Americans, with some Germans: "The Americans are extremely good and friendly, but the Germans are more industrious. The Americans compete with one another in helping the needy. If a person does not make his wants known, they come of their own accord to those they think are in need of assistance and inquire if they can be of service; but everybody in good health who is able and willing to work gets along by his own efforts."[17]

This letter caused a considerable sensation at home in Sweden. It was printed in *Östgöta Correspondenten* (Linköping), which was widely read throughout south-central Sweden, on 16 May 1846, leading to a lively debate in which anonymous persons both attacked and defended Cassel's veracity. Shortly thereafter, Cassel's letter, together with the pertinent letters to the editor, was published as a booklet of forty-eight pages in Västervik (not far from Södra Vi, Djursdala, and Odensvi parishes), giving it further publicity.[18]

The peasantry was meanwhile prepared to give full credence to Peter Cassel, a respected man of their own class, and to suspect the motives of those upper-class persons who sought to warn against emigration. The most fantastic tales about America spread through the countryside, arousing a veritable "America fever." A Småland newspaper reported in May 1846 that a beggar girl from Kisa was spreading the story that pigs in America ate their fill on raisins and almonds and drank wine from the ditches—from which it could be inferred that it was better to be a pig in America than a human being in Sweden![19]

That same year fresh groups of emigrants, mainly from Kisa and neighboring parishes, departed for Peter Cassel's New Sweden. One party of forty-two persons was misled by Cassel's letter into seeking his colony on the Des Moines River; although most of them thereafter made their way to the Cassel group, four families remained to found a new Swedish settlement at Swede Point (now Madrid), some thirty miles northwest of Fort Des Moines. Another group of seventy-five, after a hard sea voyage, was robbed of all its money in Buffalo, New York, on its way west; most of them eventually settled around Sugar Grove in northwestern Pennsylvania, which together with nearby Jamestown, New York, would in time become a center of Swedish settlement in the East; a few, however, made it to New Sweden.[20]

Needless to say, the new arrivals found the original settlers facing far harder circumstances than Peter Cassel's letter had led them to suspect, causing some disillusionment.[21] At first the settlers could only clear and cultivate small patches with spade and mattock, until they could afford a yoke of oxen which they shared in common. Agricultural prices were low, as transportation was still lacking to larger population centers, while the cost of all manufactured goods was high. Cassel's comments on the new land in a letter to his brother in Sweden dated 13 December 1848 show an indomitable though now somewhat chastened enthusiasm: "Nobody in Sweden can imagine all the advantages America offers sober, honest, and industrious persons; for them it is a veritable land of Canaan, where the natural resources are literally flowing with milk and honey. But for those who neither can nor will work, who have left Sweden with other plans for making a living, they will without exception find a Siberia, and the sooner they leave, the better, if they want to escape the greatest want and misery. Thus you see that this country can be at the same time both a Canaan and a Siberia. Truly it is a peculiar country."[22]

It was not until the fall of 1847 that Peter Cassel filed for a quarter section (forty acres) of government preemption land, at $1.25 per acre; he was the first of the New Sweden settlers to become a landowner.[23] Others followed, acquiring small holdings of usually no more than forty acres, since, as Eric Corey later recalled, "they believed it was all they needed, for in the homeland they were not used to especially large farms." Cassel and his group were later criticized for settling where they did, since much more fertile land could be had at the same price further out on the open prairie. But according to Corey, "they believed it would not work to settle or live on the prairie as there were no woods there. But almost all the Swedish pioneers had the same idea in those days." The lighter soil of the rolling, partly wooded area around New Sweden was also easier to cultivate. Early reminiscences from the settlement stress a neighborliness and cooperation at once characteristic of the American frontier and of the ancient Swedish *byalag* or rural community. Like, for instance, Bjerkeryd village in Kisa parish, from which Peter Cassel and most of his little group had come, New Sweden, too, had in its early days its own customary and unwritten law, agreed to and where necessary enforced by the inhabitants among themselves.[24]

In 1847, the same year in which Peter Cassel obtained title to his forty acres, Peter Anderson and his family—we now spell their name in the American fashion, with one s—together with Christina's younger brother, Anders Edvard Fagerström from Odensvi, who had arrived in Philadelphia aboard the *Superb* in October 1846, left New Sweden and headed west across the prairies. With them were Carl Johan Chilberg (originally Kilberg) and his family, and Sven Jacobsson, all natives of Knäred parish in Halland province, who had been Fagerström's fellow passengers on the *Superb* and reached Iowa in December. In the hilly, partly wooded country in Wapello County, some fifty miles west of New Sweden and twelve miles west of Ottumwa, they founded their own little settlement, which they called Bergholm.[25]

We may wonder why Peter Anderson decided to pull up stakes after only a little over a year in New Sweden and take land farther west. Perhaps the Andersons from Odensvi never really felt themselves a part of the close-knit group from Kisa. But one may suspect other motives. The thirty-year-old Peter had already moved many times since his poor childhood in Tryserum parish; he may well have felt less attachment both to locality and to tradition than the Kisa folk. In Odensvi he had worked on a large, rationally organized estate, unconstrained by the communal forms of the old peasant village. He may thus have been willing neither to conform to New Sweden's unwritten conventions nor to content himself with the kind of small holding its settlers deemed adequate to their modest needs. At Bergholm, Peter Anderson and C. J. Chilberg acquired several hundred acres each.[26] Thus only a few years after leaving Ogestad manor in Odensvi, Peter was very likely the owner of a larger landholding than his former master, Baron Fleetwood.

As Fagerström, Jacobsson, and the Chilbergs were only newly arrived by the beginning of 1847, it was undoubtedly Peter Anderson who had selected the site for the new settlement. It seems altogether likely that he did so quite soon after his arrival in Iowa, wrote back to Odensvi for his brother-in-law to join him, and was only waiting for Fagerström to reach New Sweden before setting off for Wapello County. It is possible that Fagerström planned from the beginning to join the Andersons as soon as a suitable location to settle was found. As the Chilbergs and Jacobsson could not have had anyone to go to in that still unsettled place, they doubtless fell in with Fagerström aboard the *Superb* and thus took part in the venture.

Bergholm was therefore the first of New Sweden's many "daughter colonies," which over the years sprang up, first in Iowa, later even farther afield in Nebraska, Kansas, and Colorado. Indeed, it was the first actual daughter colony of any of the original mother colonies settled directly from Sweden during the nineteenth century. Its establishment marks the beginning of one of the most characteristic features of the settlement of Swedes in North America: their prominent part in the westward movement. When Peter and Christina Anderson loaded their worldly goods and little daughter, Sophia, onto a wagon and headed west in 1847, they commenced a process of stage migration which in time would lead thousands of Swedish immigrants and their children to abandon the older settlements for new ones farther west.[27]

Life was hard at Bergholm in the early days. Money was in such short supply, C. J. Chilberg later recalled, that it took three years before he could afford the postage for a letter home to Sweden. He was nonetheless able to barter objects he had brought with him for a yoke of oxen, with which he claimed he had been able to break sixty acres of his own, as well as land for others, during the first summer.

Gradually the little colony grew and began to prosper. Already in 1853 Chilberg was able to travel home to Sweden for a visit.[28] He doubtless returned with a group of friends and relatives, for Bergholm's population increased rapidly for the first time both that year and the following one, with most of the new arrivals coming from Knäred parish in Halland.[29]

From the beginning, Peter Anderson was apparently the real leader of the Bergholm colony. He helped many arriving immigrants and led the community in its devotions. According to the pioneer Swedish-American historian, Pastor Eric Norelius: "The Methodists and Baptists arrived in order, as usual, to tear the congregation apart and draw the waverers to themselves, but did not succeed, which, together with the pastor's efforts, must be attributed, after God, to Peter Anderson, who took up the defense of Lutheran doctrine and in all ways sought to keep the people united in the Lutheran confession, undertook the establishment of a congregation as well as the calling of a pastor to that place, and to that end sacrificed considerable sums."[30]

The Bergholm congregation was officially founded in 1856 and Magnus Fredrik Håkanson, a former shoemaker from Stockholm who had served as New Sweden's first Lutheran pastor since 1854, accepted the call, until he moved on to Swede Bend in 1859. Peter Anderson served the new congregation as deacon, churchwarden, and sexton. His daughter Sophia was among its first six confirmands in 1858. In 1863, Peter donated five acres of his land for a church, which was ready three years later, and its surrounding cemetery. The congregation counted fifty-nine communicants by 1861 and one hundred thirteen by 1868.[31]

The Anderson family was meanwhile growing. The 1860 and 1870 censuses show that eight children—five sons and three daughters—were born between 1848 and 1868. The 1870 census also shows that one Andrew Saxe, a farm laborer, and his wife "Ingra" [*sic*], both born in Sweden and aged sixty-seven, were part of the household, very likely recent immigrants whom the Andersons were helping.

The census of 1850 meanwhile lists "Edward Fagerstren" as a resident of the county. *The History of Wapello County, Iowa*, published in 1878, shows that in that year Andrew Edward Fagerstrom—as he now called himself—was a farmer with 220 acres in Polk Township, where Bergholm was located, was married to a woman from Kentucky, had seven children, was a township trustee, treasurer of the school board, a Baptist, and a Democrat. He would appear to have quickly found his way into the mainstream of American life.[32]

Meanwhile, sometime after 1870, the Anderson family disappears from Bergholm—it is not known when or to where. The 1880 census no longer includes any of their names. The records of the Bergholm Lutheran Church would probably have provided this information, but they were lost around 1890 when its secretary's house burned down; its preserved records date only from that year and do not include the Andersons. No tombstones have been found in the cemetery for any of them. Already by the later 1860s it was noted that many people from Bergholm—or Munterville, as it soon came to be called after its Swedish-born lay preacher and schoolteacher, Magnus Munter—were leaving to settle farther west. In 1871 C. J. Chilberg and his family migrated out to the Skagit Valley in the Washington Territory, followed by a number of others from Munterville, establishing a daughter colony near La Conner.[33] It is conceivable that some or even all the Andersons found their way out there, or to some other new settlement of Munterville folk. Perhaps like many retired farm couples in the Midwest, Peter and Christina eventually moved into a nearby town, such as Ottumwa, to spend their last years, while their children dispersed to other localities. At all events it would appear that Peter Anderson's trek westward over the prairies in 1847 was not the last in his life's pilgrimage.

In 1834, seven years before Christina Lovisa Fagerström married Peter Andersson in Odensvi, her elder sister, Greta Sophia, had married a village tailor and later shopkeeper, Nils Peter Nilsson of Perstorp croft under Ogestad manor. The couple had four children, who after 1845 must have heard a great deal about their aunt and uncle and about the great land across the ocean. In 1852 the Nilssons moved to Solberga Östergård, Skede parish, in the Jönköping district of Småland. Here their elder daughter, Emma Christina Nilsdotter, then twenty-two years old, married in 1860 a man of that parish recently returned from America. Her husband, Gustaf Johnson, had gone to the United States in 1855, at the age of twenty and found his way to the Swedish settlement that had begun to grow up in the later 1840s around Andover, in Henry County, Illinois.[34]

The first group of Swedes to make their homes in Ilinois were the followers of the self-avowed prophet, Erik Jansson, eventually some eleven hundred in number, who in 1846 founded their colony, Bishop Hill, in Henry County.[35] Their enthusiastic reports from their promised land attracted growing numbers of Swedish immigrants to the area. Others, particularly from Östergötland and Småland, on their way to Peter Cassel's New Sweden in Iowa, were diverted by the Hedström brothers or by circumstance to Henry County, Illinois. In 1849 the Lutheran pastor, Lars Paul Esbjörn, fearful of the snares of Erik Jansson in Bishop Hill and of Jonas Hedström, who in 1846 had established a Swedish Methodist congregation in nearby Victoria, arrived from Sweden to found the first Swedish Lutheran congregation in the American Midwest in Andover, which now became the center of Swedish settlement in the area. In 1850 the little Andover congregation built its so-called Jenny Lind Chapel, named for the Swedish singer who was then the sensation of America and who had donated generously toward its construction. This simple brick and plaster building, surrounded by the weathered gravestones of the area's first Swedish pioneers, is revered as the "mother church" of Swedish-American Lutheranism.[36]

Gustaf Johnson spent three years in Andover, where he must have done well for himself since he was able to travel home to Sweden already in 1858. No sooner were he and Emma Christina Nilsdotter married, two years later in 1860, than they departed for America, taking with them the bride's twenty-year-old brother, Frans Viktor Nilsson. After two years in Andover, they moved early in 1862 some twenty miles to the southeast, to Altona in neighboring Knox County, where many Swedes were now settling and where the Johnsons acquired a farm. In time they achieved a certain prosperity and prominence and became pillars of Altona's Swedish Lutheran congregation. Looking ahead, they would have twelve children; two of their sons would become pastors, one of whom, Gustaf Albert (who took the name Brandelle), would serve for a number of years as president of the Augustana Synod, the Swedish Lutheran church body in America.[37]

After some four years in Illinois, Frans Viktor Nilsson meanwhile returned to Sweden in the summer of 1864. In March 1866 he married Maria Sophia Svensdotter, the eldest daughter of Sven and Sara Maria Svensson. The families were old acquaintances from Odensvi and were indeed distantly related by marriage, if not by blood.[38] Only two months later, Frans Viktor and Maria Sophia embarked for America, taking with them in turn Maria Sophia's eldest brother, Sven Fredrik, who went by the name of Westerdal.

The "America fever" was spreading and would continue to spread. But we are beginning to get ahead of our story.

4

One of Nature's Americans

We now renew acquaintanceship with a figure glimpsed fleet-
ingly at the beginning of this account. As it was long believed
that he was the first member of the clan to leave for the New
World, during the early years of the Swedish emigration, Jonas
Öhrn became shrouded with legend in the memories of later
generations. My father, in the bedtime stories he told in my
childhood, knew him only as "Captain" Öhrn, which suggested
ships and the sea. He had been in America at a very early date,
"during Andrew Jackson's time" or when Chicago was still
"Fort Dearborn"—so the story went—and had eventually returned to Sweden with a mysterious fortune, maybe even acquired through the slave trade, Dad once speculated. After
greatly impressing family and friends, he in time returned to
America. Dad later seemed to recall that he was buried somewhere near Ottumwa, in southeastern Iowa. In 1972 Clifford
Swenson in Gowrie added some new and tantalizing details to
the legend, preserved in his side of the family. Öhrn had once
owned 160 acres in what is now the center of Chicago but had
later sold it because it was "nothing but swamp and mosquitoes." Once again reference to Chicago at an early time. Then
too, Clifford claimed to have heard that Öhrn was married to an
Indian half-breed woman.

These were ideas to conjure with, especially as I learned more
about the history of the Swedes in America. Andrew Jackson
was president of the United States in 1829–37 while Fort Dear-

born was renamed Chicago in 1833. If Öhrn had been there at that time he would have been one of the very first Swedish pioneers in the Midwest, well before the Swedish immigration properly speaking, which only began after 1840. Thus over none of the *dramatis personae* in this account have I labored and speculated more during the past several years than Jonas Larsson Öhrn. My correspondence file is filled with inquiries about him to numerous persons and places in Sweden and the United States. Bit by bit I have managed to trace his footsteps and fill in the gaps.[1] If the story turns out to be somewhat less romantic than the legend, it has its epic qualities and tells us much about the earliest Swedish peasant migration to the American heartland.

The hamlet of Boda lies in the valley of a stream running out of the forested hills and down to Kyrksjön, the large "Church Lake" at the center of Odensvi parish. (The name means "Odin's cult place.") Boda consists of three farms, two of them side by side against a steep, wooded hillside. It was evidently in one of these two ancient, timbered farmsteads that Jonas Larsson was born on 2 September 1793, the first of the four children of the farmer Lars Jaensson and his wife Maria Nilsdotter. His father was the son of a landowning farmer at Österby, in neighboring Hycklinge parish, Östergötland. He had apparently come to Boda as a hired hand and in 1792 had married his master's daughter. Church records show that Jonas remained at home until his twenty-first year. The family farm, which had been in Maria Nilsdotter's family since the seventeenth century, had been a profitable one, judging from Lars Jaensson's and his wife's later prosperity and personal possessions, and Lars would surely have had much need for his oldest son's help, particularly until his two younger brothers and his sister became old enough to be useful. On New Year's Day, 1814, Maria Nilsdotter died at the age of forty-four of tuberculosis, that scourge that would carry away so many of our Odensvi ancestors. Before the year was out Lars Jaensson had taken a second wife, Brita Magdalena Hafström from Horn, a widow with three children of her own.

These developments may well have had some bearing on Jonas's leaving home that same year. In October he took employment as a *dräng*, or hired man, on a farm in neighboring Hallingeberg parish. It was customary for hired hands, both male and female, to contract their service for a year at a time, beginning in the fall, but for whatever reasons Jonas would not be bound in this fashion. During 1815 he moved twice, working on farms in Lofta and Gamleby parishes. He remained at the latter place through the following year and in 1817 appeared in the little seaport borough of Gamleby, located at the head of a long inlet from the Baltic, under a craggy, pine-clad bluff. Here he became a carpenter's helper (*snickardräng*) in the shop of Cabinetmaker Berg, adopted the surname Öhrn, and in the same year married Lena Ericsdotter, a *piga*, or hired girl, on a farm at Ullevi just south of Gamleby. A son, Lars Eric, was born to them the following year but died of measles in March 1821. Only three months later a daughter, Lena Gustafva, was born. Lena Ericsdotter died in childbirth and the child too died the same day.

Like his father, the twenty-eight-year-old widower did not long remain single. On a May day in 1822 he married Lena Cajsa Hornwall in Odensvi church. The two families had surely long been on close terms with each other; one of Jonas's eight godmothers had been born a Hornwall. Lena Cajsa was the fourth (and third surviving) of the six children of Odensvi's church organist, sexton, and schoolteacher, Daniel Hornwall, and his wife, Sara Cajsa, nee Närman, and was born on 5 March 1799 in the parish sexton's lodging near the church, which her father and grandfather had occupied since the mid-eighteenth century. That her family enjoyed considerable social standing in the area —if no great worldly wealth—is attested to by the long list of Lena Cajsa's godparents, which must have included most of the local "persons of quality," among them representatives of the clerical estate and of the noble family of Adelborg. When Lena Cajsa was only eight, her mother had died of a "consuming illness"; one once again suspects tuberculosis, of which her own mother had died in the same house thirteen years before. Daniel

Hornwall thereafter remained a widower for the rest of his long life and we may imagine that Lena Cajsa early assumed the responsibilities of the household, especially after her only sister married a farmer at Smitterstad, on the eastern edge of the parish, in 1812, at the age of fifteen.

Now Lena Cajsa had a home of her own, in Gamleby. The occupation of her bridegroom, Jonas, is listed by this time as "provision merchant" (*provisionshandlande*). When I first learned of this, the word "provision" seemed naturally enough to suggest ships' provisions, which in turn appeared to give some support to the old Öhrn legend: from being a ship's chandler in the little seaport it would not be a long step to mustering aboard a vessel bound for America "in Andrew Jackson's time" or thereabouts. I eventually learned, however, that the word *provision* in this context means "commission" in Swedish. Gamleby did not possess full municipal privileges but was a kind of subsidiary borough under the larger seaport of Västervik to the south.[2] Business in Gamleby could thus only be conducted by merchants holding burgher rights in Västervik or most frequently by "commission agents" or *provisionshandlanden* for Västervik merchants. I am told that Jonas Öhrn was unusually young to be conducting business on commission in this fashion, probably the youngest in Gamleby in his time.[3] As the little seaport's trade dealt largely with timber and other forest products, and to some degree grain, Jonas might have been in a position to exploit valuable contacts in his native parish, Odensvi. We know, for instance, that the farms at Boda operated a water-driven sawmill and a works for the rendering of pitch and stockholm tar—valuable ships' supplies—which very likely date back to that time.[4] It seems clear by this point that Jonas shared his father's enterprising nature. We may imagine him with horse and wagon, making his way over the rutted roads of northeastern Småland through woods and fields, bargaining with farmers for cattle on the hoof, grain in the sack—or its more easily transportable and marketable distilled derivative, *brännvin*, in the keg. We may picture him striding across the little cobbled square in Gamleby on his way to the quai to close a deal for salt herring in the barrel or a deckload of timber on a coastal schooner.

On 13 August 1823 Lena Cajsa gave birth to a daughter, Sara Maria. For all his efforts, meanwhile, we may wonder how well Jonas was doing with his commercial activities, for the period following the end of the Napoleonic wars in 1815, down to around 1830, was one of chronic economic recession throughout Europe, not least in Scandinavia. In any event, the Öhrns moved already in 1824 to Ullevi, just south of Gamleby, where Jonas leased a farm. In 1826 the family moved again, to Lorstad in Blackstad parish, where they also doubtless leased land until 1828. In that year they moved back to the family farm at Boda, which Jonas now took over from his father. Here Lena Cajsa gave birth to a second daughter in December 1829, who died four days later of "internal stroke." Little Sara Maria remained an only child.

Lars Jaensson did not become inactive after his son's return to Boda. The same year he and his second wife and family moved to a 4/17 *mantal* farm at Stora Skälhem in Odensvi parish, for which he eventually seems to have exchanged the farm at Boda. At his first wife Maja Nilsdotter's death in 1814 he had meanwhile inherited a quarter of a *mantal* at Smitterstad on the eastern edge of the parish, where it may be remembered that Lena Cajsa's elder sister was living, in 1832 he purchased an additional quarter of a *mantal* at the same location for the respectable sum of 4,300 *riksdaler riksgälds*. Jonas and his family moved to the Smitterstad property in 1832 to take charge. Lars Jaensson died at Stora Skälhem in 1844 of a hemorrhage, probably brought on by the old enemy, tuberculosis. As in the case of his younger contemporary, Sven Arvidsson at Karsnäs, his estate inventory gives evidence of numerous business transactions. His assets are here evaluated, after deducting various debts, at 2,230:37 *riksdaler banco*. Jonas inherited one quarter of a *mantal* at Smitterstad.

In the meantime, as we have seen, Sven Svensson had come to Smitterstad from Södra Vi, to work on Öhrn's farm. This had surely been arranged by the respective parents, for on

Sven Svenson, taken in Denver, 1889

Sven, Sara Maria, and Frida Svenson, taken in Gowrie ca. 1872–74

Sven Fredrik Westerdal, taken in Uppsala around 1892

John Svenson in his later years

Mathilda (Tilda) and Dr. C. E. Lundgren, taken in St. Paul, Minnesota, 1879

Oscar and Maria (Mary) Svenson. Wedding picture from 1893

Bullebo from "The Smithy Hill" (*Smedsbacken*), showing the old storehouse dating at least from the eighteenth century, taken in 1973

Ernest's and Jenny's first home in Portland, Oregon, 1893: on the veranda, Frida Svenson; the child in Ernest's arms is my father at the time of his christening; Jenny is on the *right*

The New Sweden Methodist Church, built in 1871, taken by Lennart Setterdahl in 1972

The Swedish Ladies' Quartette, taken in Los Angeles, 1889: *in front*, Jenny Norelius; *left*, Vilhelmina Norelius; *right*, Rina Hoving; *back*, Emmy Lindström

Jenny and Ernest Svenson (Barton) on their honeymoon in Wisconsin, 1890

Ernest with his children, Sven Hildor and Margit, around 1899

Whitsunday, 1841, which fell that year on 30 May, Sven Svensson married the daughter of the house, Sara Maria Öhrn. The new son-in-law was doubtless already a capable farmer and apparently took over the management of the farm; he even appears for a time as the owner of record of one-sixth of a *mantal* at Smitterstad.[5] In June 1842 Sara Maria gave birth to the first of their eleven children, Sven Fredrik, and in April 1844 their second child, Ludvig Daniel, was born. In 1846 the young family moved to Djursdala and established itself at Bullebo farm.

Only two years later, in July 1848, Lena Cajsa died at Smitterstad and Jonas Öhrn found himself a widower for the second time. Once again it was not long until he found himself a new wife: Johanna Westerberg, born on the island of Öland in 1812, who moved to Odensvi from Västervik in 1850. They were married in August the same year. Just one year thereafter, on 1 August 1851, Jonas sold his property at Smitterstad to a man from Västervik for 7,000 *riksdaler riksgälds*—$1,750 at the exchange rate of that time. This was close to 40 percent more than his father had paid for one quarter of a *mantal* at Smitterstad nineteen years earlier, in 1832. This increase in land values tells much about the rising pressure upon the land that would soon drive so many impoverished Swedish peasants across the sea.

No sooner did Jonas and Johanna sell their farm than they joined the early forerunners of this great movement. A fortnight later the parish register shows that they departed for North America.

We cannot but ponder why this might have been. Why should a man of fifty-eight years, newly married to a woman of thirty-nine, and proprietor of a good farm of his own, sell out, pull up stakes, and head for the prairie frontier in the American Middle West? We can only speculate. It is possible that for some reason Öhrn had come into pressing economic circumstances. Yet one suspects that the lure of the great land across the sea was the most important motive in his case, as suggested by his destination, New Sweden, Iowa.

The effectiveness of Peter Cassel's published letters is amply shown by the considerable number of persons from Odensvi,

Södra Vi, Djursdala, and other nearby parishes among the charter members of the New Sweden Lutheran Church, incorporated in May 1854.[6] Jonas and Johanna Öhrn meanwhile very likely received encouraging letters from friends or relatives already in America.

Under the circumstances it seems hard to avoid the conclusion that they were among the early cases of the "America fever" inspired by the Cassel colony in Iowa. It would remain long-lived in this old emigration area. Elsa Larsson, who was born and grew up at Boda around the turn of the century, remembers from her school years how they used to sing: "Amerika är ett härligt land, ty där växer pengar, liksom gräset växer på våra ängar [America is a glorious land, for there money grows like grass upon our meadows]."[7]

Most likely Jonas and his wife traveled as part of a group of emigrants on their way to the small Swedish settlements now established in Iowa and Illinois. If they embarked at Västervik, Karlshamn, or Gothenburg by the end of August—and they could hardly have done so any earlier—the autumn westerly gales on the Atlantic could have made their crossing a long one and a good deal more arduous than that of the Cassel party on the *Superb* in the summer of 1845.

The ship carrying the Öhrns and their fellow emigrants might have put into any one of several northern Atlantic seaports in the United States or even Canada, although it is most likely that it came to New York, sometime in the late fall of 1851. Here its passengers at last went ashore, weakened, weary, unsteady on their feet, staring in wonderment at the unfamiliar rush and bustle of the immense city and its crowded harbor.

Their journey was, however, still far from over, for their destinations lay deep in the interior of the great continent. The usual itinerary would at this time have taken them up the Hudson River on a paddle-wheeled riverboat to Albany, from there by horse-drawn barge through the Erie Canal to Buffalo, thence by steamboat through the Great Lakes to Chicago. From here, they would travel by canal boat to Peru, Illinois, then down the Illinois River to St. Louis and up the Mississippi to Fort Madison

5. The Öhrn-Hornwall family, Odensvi

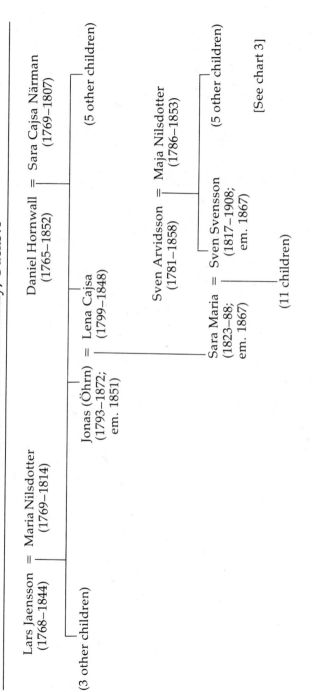

Lars Jaensson (1768–1844) = Maria Nilsdotter (1769–1814)

(3 other children)

Daniel Hornwall (1765–1852) = Sara Cajsa Närman (1769–1807)

(5 other children)

Jonas (Öhrn) (1793–1872; em. 1851) = Lena Cajsa (1799–1848)

Sven Arvidsson (1781–1858) = Maja Nilsdotter (1786–1853)

(5 other children)

[See chart 3]

Sara Maria (1823–88; em. 1867) = Sven Svensson (1817–1908; em. 1867)

(11 children)

[See chart 6]

or Burlington on the Iowa shore. From here those emigrants on their way to New Sweden would have to arrange for carts or wagons to transport themselves and their belongings the remaining forty or fifty miles across the rolling prairie to the Cassel settlement.

It may well not have been until after the turn of the new year, 1852, that Jonas reached his new home in the chill of winter. There is meanwhile no record of Johanna's having arrived with him. What happened is not clear. I once remember my father saying, with some pride, that his grandmother had "died in the shade of a covered wagon." I later discovered this was not true, for Sara Maria died in Gowrie in 1888. But it is entirely possible that Dad's memory was confused on this point and that it was Johanna Öhrn who ended her days on the last lap of the journey, practically within sight of the end of the trail. She might, like thousands of other European immigrants, have contracted cholera along the way, which was endemic during those years.

One of the most perplexing problems I faced during the first half of 1972, when my search for the family past was getting properly underway, was to find out just where in Iowa Öhrn had gone. My father seemed to recall that he was buried "somewhere near Ottumwa," in the southeastern part of the state. Clifford Swenson in Gowrie was meanwhile sure that he had heard his father say that Öhrn was buried in Munterville. In April 1972 I happened to meet Lennart Setterdahl of East Moline, Illinois, whose task it has been since 1969 to microfilm the records of Swedish congregations in North America for the Emigrant Institute in Växjö, Sweden. As chance would have it, he was going within the next couple of weeks to film the records of the Munterville Lutheran Church. Delighted at this stroke of fortune, I asked him to watch for the name of Öhrn. His efforts, alas, were in vain, for neither the church books nor the tombstones in the churchyard turned up any trace of the man we were seeking. At that point any further search seemed hopeless; to try to locate an early settler "somewhere in Iowa" would be like trying to find the proverbial needle in a haystack.

I had begun to resign myself to this frustrating impasse when

a few weeks later Lennart chanced to notice in a booklet prepared for the ninetieth anniversary of the New Sweden Methodist Church that a "Mrs. Orn" was listed among its charter
members.[8] Soon thereafter, Lennart went to New Sweden to
pick up the church records for filming. A letter arrived from
him. It contained a Xerox copy of a page from the parish register. There in faded ink was the name, "Ohrn, Jonas." It was
crossed out with heavier, later pen strokes and followed by the
notation, "died in 1872." Below it and also crossed out was
"Ohrn, Charlot, widow," followed by "removed to," with no
destination indicated. A week or two later Lennart went back to
New Sweden to return the church records. He stopped at the
old Methodist church and there the first tombstone he saw in
the churchyard—a weathered limestone slab, flat on the ground
under an overgrown lilac bush and half covered with grass and
leaves—bore the inscription: "Jonas Ohrn. Died June 15, 1872.
Aged 78 y's. 9 ms. & 13 d.," followed by an illegible reference
to "the epistle of John." "I was astounded," Lennart wrote.
Needless to say, so was I!

A year later, in September 1973, just a month after we had
visited the ancestral parishes in Småland, Aina and I drove up
to Iowa. We found New Sweden to be located a few miles north
and west of the village of Lockridge, near a place called Four
Corners, which consisted of no more than the name implied:
the intersection of two county roads with a building, in some
state of dilapidation, on each corner. A half mile to the west we
passed the overgrown Baptist burial ground, then the Lutheran
church and cemetery, and finally came to the Methodist church
and churchyard. The country is rolling and hilly, with cornfields
and pastures alternating with thickets of white oak and other
hardwoods. Apart from the churches, a quarter mile apart and
each on its own hilltop, there is and was no center to the community. Here and there is a white frame farmhouse shaded by
old elms and locusts. The old clapboard church was locked and
there was no one to let us in. After a good deal of searching,
in which we quickly found the Cassel family plot, we located
Jonas Öhrn's final resting place. Just a month before we had

seen the church where he had been christened and married. What must he not have seen and experienced between his first church visit and his last.

At the Jefferson County Courthouse in nearby Fairfield we found records that threw light upon his last twenty-one years in America. The county deed records show that 16 March 1852 —which must have been no more than a couple of months after his arrival—"Jonas Orn" purchased four parcels of land in Sections 11, 14, and 22, Lockridge Township, amounting to 170 acres in all, for $850, cash in hand. It is thus clear that whatever debts he may have had to settle in Sweden before his departure the previous summer, he arrived in America with a fatter bankroll than most of his fellow immigrants at that time. Only some two years later he paid $250, cash on the barrelhead, for a little over 90 more acres in Sections 14 and 22. And so it went. Hardly a year passed until the end of his life that Jonas did not buy or sell land, lend out money against mortgages—which sometimes brought him additional land through default—exchange properties, and so forth. After his death, his widow carried on similar business as late as 1880. The county platbook permitted us to determine with fair certainty that Öhrn's home must have been located on the south side of the east-west county road, leading from Four Corners to the New Sweden churches, just before the Baptist cemetery on the other side of the road. It may well have been one of the two frame farmhouses presently at this location.

The county marriage records meanwhile show that on 18 November 1853, "Yunos Ohrn" was married to a woman whose name, in the clerk's handwriting, appears to be "Charlotte Margreta Homo"; in the index to the same volume the last name looks more like "Homar." The recorder obviously had a difficult time with unfamiliar Swedish names and wrote them down as they sounded to him, including that of the officiating Lutheran minister, M. F. Håkanson, which he gave as "M. J. Honanson."

At the age of sixty Öhrn was now married for the fourth time, to that "Charlot" whom the New Sweden Methodist Church register had shown to be his widow. Could this be the Indian half-breed woman of the family legend? This speculation was soon settled. In Nils William Olsson's invaluable study of the Swedish immigrants who passed through New York between 1820 and 1850 I noted the arrival on the Norwegian ship *Brødrene*, from Gothenburg, of Margareta Charlotta Hammer, together with her husband, daughter, and sister, on 17 August 1849. The Jefferson County clerk could very well have mistaken her name, pronounced in the Swedish way, for "Homo" or "Homar." She had been born in Skänninge, Östergötland, in 1809. Her first husband, by whom she also had two sons not listed among the passengers on *Brødrene*, was a tanner; he must have died soon after arrival in America. Sometime after Jonas died in 1872, Charlotta left for some unknown destination, probably to live with one of her children by her first marriage. She was forty-four when she married Jonas Öhrn and they had no children together.[9]

The Iowa state census for 1856 shows that in addition to Jonas and Charlotta, their household then included her children, Alfred and Emerentia, aged eighteen and sixteen, as well as an Andrew Swanson, twenty-six, and a Mary Anderson, nineteen years old, both also natives of Sweden. Charlotta's son Amos, included in her household in the census of 1850 when he was ten, is no longer listed in 1856, nor is her sister, Gustafva Grevillius, who had then been thirty-five.[10]

Jonas and Charlotta were married by New Sweden's first lay minister, the Lutheran M. F. Håkanson. A half a year thereafter, in May 1854, Jonas was among the nineteen signers of the articles of incorporation of the New Sweden Lutheran Church. He is also noted among its first deacons. Yet by this time the community had already been stirred by the winds of doctrinal controversy. In 1849 Gustaf Unonius, now an Episcopalian missionary, had come to New Sweden, seeking to harvest souls for the denomination he was convinced most closely resembled the hierarchical and ritualistic state church in Sweden and causing "unrest," according to the Lutheran pastor. He was soon followed by the Methodist lay preacher Jonas Hedström from Victoria, Illinois, who had already made inroads among arriving Swedish Lutherans and members of Erik Jansson's millenarian sect at their colony in nearby Bishop Hill, Illinois. In 1854, the year the Lutheran church was incorporated, the Baptist missionaries, G. Almqvist and F. O. Nilsson proselytized in the neighborhood and came close to converting the Lutheran minister Håkanson himself.[11]

Peter Cassel, who had founded the colony, went over to Methodism and became its first regular lay preacher of that denomination. That Charlotta was the "Mrs. Orn" listed among the founders of the Methodist congregation at the time of Jonas Hedström's visit in the spring of 1850 is made evident by the following story about her husband, recorded by the Methodist missionary, Victor Witting, in his reminiscences:

A remarkable tabernacle meeting in New Sweden is spoken of from that time, 1855. It was the custom in our Israel to gather each year for some days in the woods and put up tents among the trees. The congregation was present in large numbers. Preachers were awaited from Illinois, but none of them arrived. The friends were discouraged and low in spirit. [The preacher Andrew] Erikson was to all intents and purposes alone in proclaiming God's word! How would it go? What might this mean? So people asked themselves. But the Lord came Himself in all His majesty to the camp, so that it was recounted for many years afterwards that a more glorious or more blessed camp meeting had never been held before in New Sweden. Among others there was a man whose name was Örn. He was a Lutheran but not converted. His wife in his second [sic] marriage was a Methodist and through her good deportment had pursuaded him to go along to the camp meeting and put up a small tent. While he was busy setting up this little tent, Örn said jokingly to the Methodists, "This is not large, but it will have to house two congregations." Erikson preached on the text: "He that goeth forth and weepeth, bearing precious seed, shall doubtless come again with rejoicing, bringing his sheaves with him" Psalms 126:6. The Lord made manifest His servant's words: Örn lay as though struck by lightning and cried out to God for salvation. His cry was heard—and the tent he had put up now housed only *one* congregation. Örn was thereafter a true and helpful member of the Methodist congregation right up until his death.

The Lutheran sources limit themselves to the curt statement that Öhrn "became a Methodist." [12]

The two churches and three burial grounds, all within a radius of less than half a mile, at the little New Sweden settlement provide a reminder of that fierce denominational rivalry that so soon came to characterize so many Scandinavian frontier communities in the last century. [13] In 1858 the colony consisted of some five hundred persons, to some degree interspersed among their neighbors of old American and German background, yet four years earlier this Swedish group was already divided into Lutheran, Methodist, and Baptist congregations. [14] It is difficult for us today to comprehend the doctrinal controversies of that time and even more the significance attached to them by these people of much faith but little book learning. Still, they provide the key to much that was most characteristic of their mentality. Without understanding the role that church and sect played in their lives, we cannot glimpse the lost world of their values, hopes, and dreams.

Traditionally the Christian faith has held that this earthly life is a "vale of tears," that those who bear its burdens with meekness and humility may, if God in His wisdom and mercy sees fit to grant the gift of grace, receive their reward in the eternal life to come, and that to covet the things of this world is to worship false idols. The Christian was thus taught obedience to existing authority, spiritual and worldly, and acceptance of the apparent inequities of this temporal existence.

By the early nineteenth century, however, the new secular ideal of progress in this world of the here and now began to filter down from the classes to the masses, spreading the belief that one should not accept poverty and injustice but rather strive to improve one's lot in life. This aroused a reaction against the old orthodoxy, not only on the part of freethinkers and agnostics but among a multitude of believers as well, giving rise to new, individualistic doctrines of salvation. These taught the necessity of that personal repentance of which Jonas Öhrn provided so edifying an example. At the same time they generally saw no contradiction between success in worldly enterprises and membership in the company of the elect; honest prosperity was indeed taken as a sign of divine grace. Both the Scandinavian countries and North America experienced by midcentury a great "awakening" of individualistic pietism.[15]

The immigrants of this time exemplify the interaction of secular and religious currents. They were manifestly committed to the belief in improvement in their material conditions through individual effort. At the same time they could hardly have made the sacrifices and faced the hardships they did without their inherited faith in the far better life to come, in which they would be eternally reunited with those loved ones they might never hope to see on this earth again. The harsh conditions of frontier life impressed these pioneers both with the need for self-reliance and the urgency for finding the sure path to salvation. Standing amid the timeworn slabs and obelisks of the old burial grounds here on the rolling, windy Midwestern grasslands, one senses something of their quiet courage and restless faith.

Jonas could well rejoice in the bounty of his Lord. He probably farmed on some scale, taking advantage of the plentiful and cheap source of labor provided by the constant arrival in New Sweden of sturdy young countrymen anxious to earn the means to go into farming for themselves. The Andrew Swanson and Mary Anderson, shown as part of his household in the 1856 census, were probably hired help of this kind. But at his age and with his resources his main economic activity would seem to have been his various land transactions. Although the records on hand are evidently incomplete—they do not show, for instance, what property the widow Hammer might have brought into the marriage or what land Öhrn might have bought or sold outside Jefferson County—they indicate that he bought most of his acreage during his first two years in New Sweden, in large parcels at low prices, ranging from $2.78 to $5.00 per acre, and thereafter sold land in smaller parcels at higher prices ranging up to $25.00 per acre, or in one instance two acres at $125.00 each.

Land prices rose as the population of the area grew—during 1857, for instance, New Sweden's increased by fully one-sixth— and with the building of the Burlington and Missouri Railroad through the area in the later 1850s. A report on the New Sweden settlement in *Hemlandet, det Gamla och det Nya*, the first regular Swedish newspaper in the United States, founded in 1855 and at that time still published in Galesburg, Illinois, stated in 1858 that of one hundred Swedish families in the New Sweden settlement at that time, eighty-six owned a total of 5,065 acres (which would average about 59 acres each), of which 1,788 under cultivation. Only one family, not named, possessed over 200 acres; it is evident that this must have been the Öhrns, who the county records show held 263 acres in that year. According to the census of 1860, "John Orn" owned property evaluated at $1,500 in real estate plus $200 in personal estate. That same census showed not more than four or five persons in Lockridge Township with higher property evaluations. Ten years later, in 1870, the census reveals that "Jonas Irn" or "Iren" still possessed $500 in farm property, which included $80 worth of livestock and an unspecified amount in implements. His total acreage is not given but it is noted that it now included "4 improved acres." He also had $980 in personal estate.[16]

We may meanwhile imagine Öhrn involved in a variety of other activities. We have seen that he made numerous loans against mortgages and at good interest. He may also have traded in grain, livestock, and other commodities. He was, according to Victor Witting, a "useful" member of his Methodist congregation and he may well have played his part in arranging for the construction of the present clapboard church building in 1871, which replaced the old log church begun in 1854.[17]

Not long before this, in 1868, New Sweden's Lutheran lay

minister, Håkan Olson wrote: "When I came here [in 1858] our countrymen had not been able to cultivate very much around their homes. Most of the land was covered by brush. Many had debts greater than what their pieces of land were worth; some left and went to Illinois. The Lord, however, soon gave us better times. The dilligence and industry of our countrymen is talked of and admired by our neighbors. . . . Whoever saw our settlement ten years ago will now hardly recognize it. There are now large, well-tilled fields where before there were bushes and thickets; in place of the small log cabins you will now find fine frame houses. Some have fine, large orchards and vinyards, and, best of all in the temporal sense, most of them have paid off their debts."[18]

A little over a year before he died, Jonas Öhrn made out his will on 9 March 1871. He signed it with an X, which suggests a paralyzing stroke, and it was witnessed by A. F. Cassel and F. O. Danielson.[19] He bequeathed all his property to his wife, after whose death any money still loaned out at interest should go to his daughter, Sara Maria Svenson, who by now was in Iowa.

In America we have tended to conceive of the European immigrant as the hapless victim of forces beyond his own control, rudely uprooted out of a secure and unchanging peasant society and thrown into the turmoil of a new world in the midst of rapid and often reckless development.[20] However true this pattern may have been for emigrants from some parts of Europe, it scarcely fits the life of Jonas Öhrn up to his departure at the age of fifty-eight. My extensive study of Swedish church records from the first half of the nineteenth century amply bears out recent research in Sweden indicating a high degree of mobility among the country's rural population during this period, greater indeed than in much of the second half of the century.[21]

Given such conditions, the readiness of many Swedish peasants to face the great unknown across the Atlantic by the middle of the century seems more understandable. It has been said of them that they were American in spirit before they ever left home.[22] The restless, mobile, enterprising career of Jonas Lars-son Öhrn, from the time he first left the family hearth at the age of twenty-one, seems to show that he had long been one of Nature's Americans and that he must have fitted into the free-wheeling world of the prairie West without regrets and with scarcely a backward glance.

5

The Master of Bullebo

Our scene shifts in place and time, back to Bullebo farm in
Djursdala parish, where Sven Svensson, his wife Sara Maria,
and their two small sons established themselves in 1846. Bullebo
farmstead lies at the end of an alley of birches, on the slope of
a hill, from the crest of which—the "Smithy Hill" (Smedsback-
en)—a magnificent panorama unfolds itself. From the far side of
the hill plowlands and meadows extend down to the reedy shore
of Lake Juttern, beyond the southern end of which Djursdala
church with its separate belfry is seen on its hilltop above the
fields. Steeper slopes rise on the far side of the narrow lake,
which stretches far out of sight to the north, amid forested headlands and ridges, blue in the distance. Looking eastward from
the "Smithy Hill," over the rooftops of the farm, the birch alley,
and the stony pastures on either side, one sees how the forest
narrowly confines this northern edge of the parish's settled and
cultivated core along the lakeshore.

The farm was of course an ancient one and its standing within
the parish is shown by its once having been the residence of the
local *länsman*, or king's sheriff. In 1815, Sven's father, Sven
Arvidsson of Karsnäs, Södra Vi, bought a quarter of a *mantal*
at Bullebo, to which he added another quarter *mantal* through
purchase in 1840. As no member of his family lived at Bullebo
until Sven moved there from Odensvi in 1846, Sven Arvidsson
doubtless leased out these holdings during the intervening
years. In 1847, the year after Sven Svensson's arrival, his father
gave one quarter of a *mantal* at Bullebo each to him and to his
younger brother, Carl Johan, who had already acquired prop-

erty through marriage at Stora Flarka in Horn, Östergötland, not far to the north, where he was also an innkeeper.

Bullebo, consisting at this time of two farms with several *torp*, or small tenancies, under them, was still officially a "village" (*by*) and one, moreover, still organized in the age-old manner with the small fields and pastures and larger forest allotments belonging to the landowners of the village divided and interspersed, even to some extent with the holdings of inhabitants of the neighboring villages of Hallersrum to the south and Björkesnäs to the north. Since 1803 laws had been passed in Sweden permitting the reallocation of village lands by local agreement to form more rational, contiguous landholdings. In 1854 the two Svensson brothers redivided Bullebo in accordance with the law of 1827 (*laga skifte*); it was as a result of this agreement that Sven retained the old farmstead while Carl Johan received the big house itself.[1] As we have seen, he moved it to Horn, where it served for a time as an inn. Its stone foundations may still be seen on the grassy hillside between and a little above the old wing buildings at Bullebo. Sven and his family occupied, now if not before, the two-story building on the south side of the house lot.

To know that Sven owned a farm of one quarter of a *mantal* tells us nothing about the actual area of his holdings. It would appear, however, from later information that it amounted to around 400 *tunnland*, or about 480 acres, most of it forest, about equally divided between Bullebo itself and the separate Långasjö farm in the forest some distance to the northeast, near the Östergötland boundary.[2] We can gain some further sense of scale from Vilhelm Moberg's description of the typical Småland parish of Ljuder in 1846—the year Sven Svensson moved to Bullebo—in which two-thirds of the landholdings consisted of one-eighth of a *mantal* or less; as in Moberg's Ljuder too, it is likely that more than half of Djursdala's population neither owned nor leased farms or regular tenancies (*torp*), but were landless farm laborers.[3]

The decade of the 1850s was a promising time for those with land and resources in Sweden. Forests were beginning to offer increasing possibilities for commercial exploitation beyond the supply of building material and fuel for local use, as shown by the modest sawmill and the pitch and tar works at Boda. Yet more important at this time was grain cultivation. Bullebo included some good arable land by the lake. Making use of new methods of cultivation then being propagated by provincial agricultural improvement societies its yields could be increased. The farm moreover, contained extensive bogs and marshlands which could be made fertile and productive if properly ditched and drained. As the prices for wheat, rye, and oats rose between 20 and 30 percent through the decade, land sales and speculation increased markedly, with an accompanying rise in land values. Land purchases and agricultural improvements meanwhile led to the increasing use of credit, both from individuals and the new mortgage associations of the period.[4]

Sven Svensson, the son of Sven Arvidson and son-in-law of Jonas Öhrn, was not behindhand in seeking to grasp the opportunities of the times. The first important step toward the more rational and profitable exploitation of his land was its consolidation through redivision of the property with his brother, Carl Johan. The year 1854 was a highly propitious time for such an undertaking, for the outbreak of the Crimean War was just then cutting western Europe off from the Russian grain from Black Sea ports upon which it was becoming increasingly dependent. Sven now undertook an ambitious project for the draining and cultivating of bogs and marshes. He seems also to have had plans for lowering the level of a small lake to reclaim the land around its shore, and to build a water-driven mill.[5]

By all indications Sven did well during the mid and later 1850s. Sara Maria was able to decorate the house—about which we will have more to say later. The family and its dependents from Bullebo occupied by tradition the third pew in Djursdala church of a Sunday, except for Sven, who as a churchwarden (*kyrkvärd*) sat on the bench reserved for such dignitaries in the front of the church. In the spring of 1853, his eldest son, Sven Fredrik, then eleven years old, was enrolled in the intermediate school (*lägre läroverk*) in Vimmerby. The family meanwhile continued to grow apace. The third child and first daughter, Maria Sophia, was born at Bullebo in 1846, the year of the family's arrival there. Johan Theodor followed in 1848, then Matilda in 1851, Arvid Fritjof in 1853, Oscar Henrik in 1856. My grandfather, Ernst Otto, was born in 1859, followed by Emil Seth in 1861, Frida Viktoria in 1864, and finally Lovisa Elisabeth in 1866.

Yet beneath this apparent prosperity there were mounting problems. Sven's innovations badly strained his relations with his neighbors. Prior to 1854, Bullebo's lands were partly mixed up with those of the neighboring villages, with isolated holdings on either side. In carrying through the reallocation, Sven sought to eliminate such enclaves through exchange, which aroused the bitter resistance of the villagers, who were fearful of losing ancient landholdings for property they feared might be of inferior quality. Sven's drainage project involved watercourses passing through the properties of a number of Hallersrum's smallholders while the planned watermill would require diverting the flow of a stream, to the evident advantage of the master of Bullebo, but not of the villagers. Or so they apparently felt.

These conflicts were wearisome and frustrating to Sven and his family. "Madame Svensson" is still remembered to have said before they left for America, "I have been caught here between Björkesnäs and Hallersrum for so long that now I want to get away!" [6] On the villagers' side the situation created such an impression that it has by no means been forgotten among their descendants even now, for behind the specific points at issue there loomed far greater implications. Sven Svensson, despite his family's long association with Bullebo, was a "stranger," from out of parish. The designation of his wife as "Madame," whether applied in grudging respect or in irony, suggests a certain social distance between the Svenssons of Bullebo and their neighbors that could well give rise to envy and suspicion.

But more important still, Sven, like his father and father-in-law, belonged to a new breed in the Swedish countryside, who looked at farming as a profitable form of investment and speculation, and no longer simply as a way of life, traditional and unchanging. The new master of Bullebo threatened, in effect, to undermine the cherished ways passed on by one generation to the next since time immemorial. In other parts of Sweden at that time land reallocations were advancing rapidly, breaking up the old compact villages with their largely communal way of life and forcing many of their inhabitants to move out to the isolation of their new, consolidated farms. The social and psychological implications of this drastic restructuring of the old agrarian society were profound.[7] The conservatism of Djursdala and nearby parishes in northeastern Småland is shown by the fact that reallocation came late and resulted in only a very limited degree of consolidation in a number of villages. My friend Gösta Karlsson, who leases three farms in Djursdala village, told me in 1973 that these consist of some thirty separate pieces of ground in some ten different locations. Björkesnäs, Hallersrum, and Djursdala village, near the parish church, have remained compact villages of the old type down to the present day. Under such circumstances it is understandable that the enterprising Sven should encounter obstacles at every turn while his natural impatience with his neighbors probably did nothing to heal the rift.

This, however, was not all, for with time Sven faced mounting financial difficulties. It is not known what debts or obligations he might have assumed upon taking over the farm, although we know that property transfers at that time were frequently burdened in this fashion. There were legal, surveying, and enclosure costs in connection with the division of the Bullebo lands. Above all the ambitious drainage and land reclamation project required a sizable investment which could be returned only when the new land became productive and if grain prices remained high. To implement his plans Sven undoubtedly incurred debts. By 1857, however, grain prices began to decline. Credit became more difficult to obtain and interest rates rose. By 1864 overindebtedness on the part of cultivators combined with overextended lending by mortgage associations had led to a financial crisis resulting in numerous business failures, defaults, and foreclosures.[8]

"We became poor before we went to America," Johan Svensson—who now called himself John—recalled at the end of his long life; his further comments suggest that this caused them to be treated with some condescension by their relatives.[9] For the proud master of Bullebo this was intolerable. He found himself up against a painful dilemma: if he stayed on his farm he would not only have to give up his ambitious plans for improvement but would probably have to sell much of his property to settle his debts, thereby compromising the future prospects in life of his eleven children. If, meanwhile, he sold out altogether, he could obtain the means to transport his family to America and there acquire a sizable tract of fertile land to make a fresh start under far more promising circumstances. It was not so much actual poverty as the fear of poverty and the social degradation it would bring that impelled him to make the decision he did.

There are apparent indications of the family's growing difficulties. The eldest son, Sven Fredrik, who had been studying in Stockholm during 1857–58 in preparation for a clerical calling, broke off his studies around 1859 to teach school in Kristdala, Småland. In June 1864 the second son, Ludvig, departed for America; Sven paid his passage so that he might investigate possibilities for the rest of the family.[10]

My father evidently knew nothing of these economic problems. It had meanwhile been his understanding that the Svenssons had come to America largely out of dissatisfaction with religious conditions in Sweden. This I found confirmed by one of John Svenson's later reminiscences. Speaking of one Tora Turnell, daughter of his godmother, the Djursdala pastor's wife, he recalled in 1930: "I danced with her and her sister Emily when we were small children, but then . . . my parents and brothers and sisters became 'readers' (though it did not take very much on me). The Turnells became less friendly toward us, which does not surprise me now."[11] The term "readers" (läsare) meant pietists, with reference to their stress upon individual reading of the Bible as the source of literal truth. When John revisited his birthplace in 1928 he recognized the wallpaper in one of the upstairs rooms and could clearly remember when it had been put up seventy years earlier.[12] This would have

6. The children of Sven and Sara Maria Svensson, 1842–1935

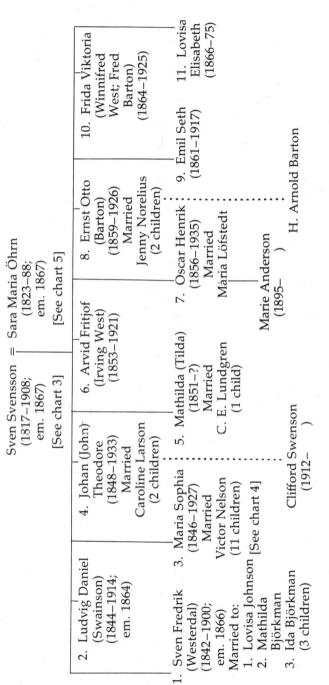

Sven Svensson = Sara Maria Öhrn
(1817–1908; (1823–88;
em. 1867) em. 1867)
[See chart 3] [See chart 5]

2. Ludvig Daniel (Swainson) (1844–1914; em. 1864)

4. Johan (John) Theodore (1848–1933)
Married
Caroline Larson
(2 children)

6. Arvid Fritjof (Irving West) (1853–1921)

8. Ernst Otto (Barton) (1859–1926)
Married
Jenny Norelius
(2 children)

10. Frida Viktoria (Winnifred West; Fred Barton) (1864–1925)

1. Sven Fredrik (Westerdal) (1842–1900; em. 1866)
Married to:
1. Lovisa Johnson [See chart 4]
2. Mathilda Björkman
3. Ida Björkman
(3 children)

3. Maria Sophia (1846–1927)
Married
Victor Nelson
(11 children)

5. Mathilda (Tilda) (1851–?)
Married
C. E. Lundgren
(1 child)

7. Oscar Henrik (1856–1935)
Married
Maria Löfstedt

9. Emil Seth (1861–1917)

11. Lovisa Elisabeth (1866–75)

Clifford Swenson
(1912–)

Marie Anderson
(1895–)

H. Arnold Barton

NOTE: Broken lines indicate descent without showing intervening generations.

been around 1858, when the family was apparently at the peak of its fortunes. The wallpaper—I have a sample—was doubtless expensive, represented the height of fashion, and would surely have been condemned by the pietists as a worldly vanity. This small detail helps us to date the family's conversion sometime after 1858.

But why just at this time? Already during the 1830s and 1840s the province of Småland in particular had been swept by waves of evangelistic pietism, giving rise to scenes of exhaltation in which participants fell into trances and "talked in tongues."[13] This movement had quite evidently left the Svenssons and their relatives untouched.

The most obvious source of inspiration would seem to have been the oldest son of the family, Sven Fredrik. At the pastor's annual household visitations (*husförhör*) he had received top marks in reading and Christian knowledge, and in 1853, as seen, he was sent to Vimmerby to continue his education at the intermediate school. At that time a peasant boy rarely received any schooling beyond the rudiments of literacy unless he were destined for the clergy. Already in 1835, seven years before Sweden's School Law of 1842, the parishioners of Södra Vi voted to support a parish schoolmaster, although implementation lagged thereafter. In the same year a similar proposal was decisively voted down in the smaller and poorer Djursdala parish. In accordance with the School Law, however, an itinerant schoolteacher was eventually engaged there, who instructed neighborhood children for periods of two or three weeks each year at selected farms throughout the parish. Gösta Karlsson told me in 1973 that his grandfather had "gone two years, three weeks a year, to an itinerant schoolmaster." Aside from such instruction as they could pick up from the older members of their household and from "reading" for confirmation, this would also have been the extent of the schooling provided for the Svensson children, for Djursdala's first permanent schoolhouse, next to the church, was not built until 1872, after they had emigrated.[14]

To have a son in the pastorate was, however, a natural goal for socially ambitious peasant families like the Svenssons. Yet the prospects for such "peasant students" were not bright, for the available positions in the state church were largely monopolized by the old, established clerical families. In their frustration many disappointed aspirants turned their criticisms against the condition of the church and its clergy, many of whom were indeed ripe targets for attack because of their worldly, perfunctory, and complacent attitudes toward their call. The would-be reformers expounded a deeper personal commitment to the faith, uncompromising standards of Christian morality among clergy and laity alike, and the literal interpretation of scripture.

During 1857–58 we find Sven Fredrik, after completing three years in Vimmerby, attending Pastor Peter Fjellstedt's school in Stockholm, where young men of modest educational background prepared for the demanding *studentexamen*, or qualifying examinations, required for study at the university theological faculties. Having missed his scheduled confirmation at home through illness he was confirmed in Stockholm's so-called German Church in 1858. For whatever reasons, he did not continue at the school, but after Fjellstedt's associate, Pastor A. P. Ahlberg, left Stockholm to establish his own school for lay preachers and missionaries at Kristdala (later Ahlsborg) in Småland, Sven Fredrik, still in his teens, had the chance to join him and teach for a time at the new school. Both Fjellstedt and Ahlberg exerted a powerful influence upon the pietist movement and from their schools went forth many young men who would later serve in the Swedish-American ministry. [15]

The pietists were not generally rebels against the church itself but sought rather to bring about its regeneration from within. They were nonetheless regarded with mistrust and distaste by most of the church establishment. Those younger clerics who sympathized with pietism often found themselves under a cloud with their superiors and frustrated in their careers. Some of these therefore went to America to work among their countrymen, thereby imparting to Swedish Lutheranism in the New World a distinctly more democratic, low-church, evangelical, and puritanical character than the mother church in Sweden.[16] Sven Fredrik and his friends must have followed with excitement and envy the reports of these pioneer pastors' successes in the Lord's vineyard.[17]

One surmises that it was sometime after Sven Fredrik's return from Stockholm in 1858 that his pietism began to impress itself upon his family. Not only did they naturally share in his vocational disappointments but increasingly they faced setbacks of their own. To even the conventionally religious a reversal of earthly fortunes may appear as an admonition from on high to seek the path of righteousness while there is yet time. That Sven at this point may have felt he had something to repent is suggested in a letter from John Svenson in 1929. "The sons of Karsnäs," he wrote, "were not so faultless. They surely liked *brännvin* a little too well. At their get-togethers they had plenty of fun all right, drank and got tipsy. I should not have written in this way about my relatives and father, but it is true that some of them went too far with some things."[18]

Tradition holds that the first private prayer meetings in Djursdala parish were held at the remote forest tenant farms, Bäckafall and Kvarntorpet, which belonged to Bullebo.[19] The home farm itself soon became the center of pietism in the neighborhood. "Then came Oscar Ahnfelt, Fjellstedt, Stackelberg, and other 'pious' preachers," John recalled.[20] Ahnfelt was an immensely popular gospel singer and lay preacher. Count Adolf Stackelberg was the founder of the Northeast Småland Mission Society, which is still active today; as his manor, Stensnäs, was in Ukna parish near Odensvi, it is likely that he was acquainted with the Hornwall family. Fjellstedt we have encountered already.

"I recall," John wrote on another occasion, "we were called the 'Bullebo Readers,' certainly not without reason, for if any preacher came along he could naturally stay at Bullebo—Ahlberg, Nylander, Tulander, pastors and also some colporteurs."[21]

If Pastor Tornell in Djursdala was disconcerted by his churchwarden's conversion to pietistic beliefs, we may well imagine the reaction of the pastor's immediate superior, the redoubtable Doctor of Theology Arvid Moberger, dean (*kontraktsprost*) of neighboring Södra Vi, a man of unshakable orthodoxy and a paternalistic autocrat of the old school. Of him the following exchange is reported when one of his parishioners once sought to remonstrate with him: "Who has baptized you? 'You, Herr Doktor.' Who has confirmed you? 'You did, Herr Doktor.' Who has married you? 'You, Herr Doktor.' Who has buried your parents? 'You, Herr Doktor.' Who has baptized your children? 'Herr Doktor.' Who has confirmed your children? 'You, Herr Doktor.' All right, sit down and be quiet." [22] Moberger had been pastor at Södra Vi since 1832 and had known the Svenssons since Sven had been a boy in his teens. He must have watched developments at Bullebo with bitterness in his heart.

In March 1866—as we have noted earlier—Sven and Sara Maria's eldest daughter, Maria Sophia, married Frans Viktor Nilsson from Solberga in Skede parish. The bridegroom had been born in Odensvi parish in 1840, thus his family had doubtless long known the Öhrn-Hornwall-Svensson clan. Victor Nelson, as he now called himself, had been in Andover, Illinois, from 1860 to 1864. A month after moving to Solberga, Victor and Sophia left for America, in June 1866. With them went Sophia's eldest brother, Sven Fredrik, who as noted now called himself Westerdal.

By this time there can be little doubt that Sven Svensson was already making plans to bring the rest of the family over to the new land. The departure of Victor, Sophie, and Sven Fredrik must have been preceded by long and serious discussions on the subject. Sven must by now have been fairly well informed about America and its possibilities. His father-in-law, Jonas Öhrn, had been in America for fifteen years and his second son, Ludvig, for the past two years. Yet even before Öhrn had left in 1851 there had been much talk of America. Sven and his family had still been living at Smitterstad, Odensvi, on Öhrn's farm, when Victor's aunt and uncle, Christina and Peter Andersson, whom they surely knew, had departed for America in 1845. We can imagine how intently Sven and Jonas must have discussed this venture and the news from the Cassel colony at

New Sweden, Iowa, to which Öhrn himself would emigrate not long after. Other threads tie Peter Cassel's Kisa emigrants of 1845 to Sven's own home parish of Södra Vi. In 1928, the Swedish-American historian, George M. Stephenson—whose own family had emigrated from Södra Vi to New Sweden, Iowa— met one Elof Gustafsson in Örsåsa village, Södra Vi, whose father, Gustaf Jakobsson, had transported the Cassel party on the first lap of their journey to Gothenburg. Sven's eldest brother, Nils Johan, had owned property in Örsåsa since 1839 and the Svenssons were probably well acquainted with Gustaf Jakobsson. It was from Örsåsa, too, that the first family from Södra Vi parish departed for America in 1846, the year Sven and his family moved to Bullebo in Djursdala. It is not impossible that they were among those who gathered to see Samuel Jönsson and his family off on their adventurous voyage. Thereafter no persons from Södra Vi took out emigrant passes for the next three years, but letters and reports from the New World had their effect, as evidenced by the forty-three persons who left the parish for America in 1849, in which year there was a notable upsurge in emigration from the surrounding parishes as well. Among the 1849 emigrants from Södra Vi was Steffan Steffansson, Professor Stephenson's grandfather and a distant relative of Sven Svensson, who despite his family's severe tribulations on the voyage, sent home a hopeful report from New Sweden, Iowa.[23]

The first emigrant from Djursdala of whom I have any record went to Henry County, Illinois, from Björkesnäs—which adjoined Bullebo to the north—in 1849.[24] Throughout the years that followed, all the parishes we have spoken of here, including Odensvi, Södra Vi, and Djursdala, continued to contribute a proportionately high share of the early Swedish emigration. Increasing numbers of America-letters reached more and more homes in the area and were avidly read, passed around the neighborhood, copied, and sometimes published in provincial newspapers. Good times for Swedish agriculture by the mid-1850s, followed by the American Civil War, slowed the pace of emigration for some years, but after the end of the war in 1865 emigration once again increased.

What might I not give to unearth in some old attic a cache of letters to Sven Svensson from his father-in-law and later, from his three eldest children and son-in-law in America! The hope is always there. Surely such letters—together with Victor Nelson's firsthand accounts of America—must have been of crucial importance as the great decision was reached at Bullebo. On 14 March 1867 Sven sold his farm to his relative Johan Gustaf Olsson of Slitshult, Södra Vi, grandfather of Bullebo's present owner, Nils Olsson, for 13,600 *riksdaler riksmynt* or $3,400 at the exchange rate of the time. Långasjö was sold separately to a certain Johansson in Hallersrum; its present owners are related to us.[25] Before the year was over he would have cause to thank Providence that he had sold when he did, for 1867 turned out to be the first of two years of disastrous crop failures that would send impoverished Swedish farmers to America in hitherto unprecedented numbers in 1868 and 1869.[26]

Sven would now have had to secure an emigration permit for himself, his wife, and eight children, most probably from Dean Moberger in Södra Vi. We can well imagine the latter's vain efforts to dissuade this stiff-necked and errant member of his flock from forsaking the earthly home that God had given him. It was to no avail.[27] At the end of the year Dean Moberger had to list the names of this part of an old and respected local family on his annual report of emigrants to "North America" from Djursdala parish.

The fateful day approached. On 14 June the Svensson family was officially removed from the Djursdala parish register. They probably departed a few days later. The graveled yard in front of the house was surely filled with friends and relatives that June morning. The fields were green with growing rye and oats, and the lilacs were in full bloom. The story is still told in Djursdala that when the wagons were loaded with the family and their belongings, the former master of Bullebo bared his head and prayed aloud to God that the doors of this house never be closed to God's Word. It is related that the Lord answered this prayer and that Bullebo has always been inhabited by God-fearing folk since that day.[28] Sven Svensson mounted the lead wagon. He and his family drove out through the gate and down the birch alley for the last time. He was in his fiftieth year. A new world and a new life awaited.

6

Fresh Beginnings on the Prairie

By 1867 conditions of travel had changed remarkably since Peter Anderson's family and Jonas and Johanna Öhrn had set forth for America in the 1840s and 1850s. No longer need the departing emigrants trek overland with hired teams and wagons to some possibly distant seaport, in search of a vessel taking on cargo and passengers for some North American destination, and there to bargain with its captain over the terms of passage. Means of transport by both land and sea were now greatly improved and the Atlantic emigrant traffic highly organized.

During the years of the American Civil War, British and to a lesser degree German shipping companies, liberally subsidized by their governments, undertook an ambitious program of steamship construction in anticipation of heavy emigrant traffic following the end of the war. After 1865 the overwhelming majority of Atlantic passengers traveled by steam and the era of sail in the history of the emigration was over. Steam propulsion not only reduced the time required for the crossing but also permitted regular, scheduled departures and arrivals, little affected by the vagaries of wind and weather. As the new steamships were built to carry passengers it became essential for the shipping firms to assure themselves of a large and relatively steady demand to keep them filled. This led to the rapid organization of a network of agencies throughout much of western and central Europe, not least in Scandinavia, and cartel arrangements that reserved the emigrant traffic from different parts of the

Continent for the principal British and German lines. Scandinavia fell essentially into the British sphere. The leading British passenger lines had their agents located in the larger Swedish ports, above all Gothenburg, who in turn had subagents in provincial towns throughout the country. These latter publicized their respective shipping firms within their localities and often, by agreement, various American railroads as well. It must therefore have been easy enough for Sven Svensson to acquire information about travel arrangements and even to book passage for himself and his family from Gothenburg to his final destination in the United States by scheduled conveyance before leaving home, most probably though a subagent in Vimmerby. The same month the Svenssons left Djursdala, Victor Nelson's older brother, Johan August Nilsson, a farmer from Solberga Östergård, Skede parish, also departed for America with his family and it seems natural to suppose that the two families joined company en route.[1]

It is not absolutely certain which route the Svenssons followed on their way to America, but we may reasonably assume that they took the now established one traveled by the great majority of their fellow emigrants by that time. Their first destination would thus have been Gothenburg. Sweden's great western seaport had just within the past few years become far more accessible to emigrants from the hinterland thanks to the railroad construction of the middle 1860s: the opening of the Western Trunkline from Stockholm to Gothenburg in 1864 and of the Southern Trunkline, which branched off from the former at Falköping and led south through Småland to Malmö, in 1866. The Svenssons would thus have traveled by wagon some fifty-odd miles west to Nässjö, there taking leave of the returning teamsters, their last farewell to old friends and neighbors. Here they would have boarded a train—surely a new and exciting experience for all of them—traveled north to Falköping and, transferring there, west to Gothenburg.

The cobbled streets of Gothenburg were filled with lumbering carts piled high with the "America-trunks" of departing emigrants and with raw-boned peasant families, awkward in their

Sunday best, thronging the shipping agencies or window-shopping in unaccustomed idleness while waiting to embark upon the great adventure of their lives.

Here our emigrants would board one of the vessels of the Wilson Line, which monopolized traffic on this first lap of the voyage, and dropping down the Göta River into the open water of the Kattegat, watched the rockbound coastline fall below the horizon—the last most of them would ever see of the land of their birth.

As our travelers had never before ventured out onto the ocean wave, let us hope that the North Sea was not then as rough as it has a well-earned reputation for being, even at that relatively favorable time of year. After some three days they would have landed at Hull, on the northeast coast of England, and from there traveled by rail across the northern Midlands to Liverpool, the great terminus for the Atlantic traffic. Like most of their countrymen who left accounts of the journey, they were surely impressed by the green, well-tended countryside through which they passed with such disconcerting speed, but dismayed by the grime and coal smoke of Liverpool.[2]

After possibly a wait of a few days they would have boarded their ship, belonging to the Inman, Anchor, White Star, or other British line, in the roadstead and headed down the Mersey estuary into the open sea, stopping possibly at Queenstown in Ireland to take on emigrants before setting course across the Atlantic for New York.

Conditions of ocean travel had improved so greatly that a woman in New Sweden, Iowa, who had emigrated from Sweden in the 1850s, would write in 1868 that the crossing was "a pleasure trip compared to what it was in former days."[3] We would be less inclined to think so today. The steamships of the 1860s were still of only modest tonnage compared with the majestic liners of the end of the century and were still stabilized and partly propelled by sail. Living and feeding arrangements were spartan but adequate for emigrants unused to many of the comforts and amenities of life: the accommodations were designed for passengers, who no longer had to provide their own bedding and provisions. Best of all, the crossing from Liverpool to New York now took only ten to twelve days; the record crossing for 1867 took nine days, six hours.[4]

Making their journey during the early summer, the Svenssons probably enjoyed good weather at least most of the way across. We may thus picture the various emigrant groups foregathered in their accustomed areas on deck conversing in a babel of tongues of the familiar past and the unknown future, spinning yarns or listening in awed silence to the boasting of some "old American," returning from a visit to the old country at the head of a little band of relatives and friends, playing cards to the accompaniment of much cheerful profanity, flirting in odd corners, and dancing to the tune of fiddle or concertina. We can imagine too, the fascination of the younger Svenssons with all this colorful life going on around them and the efforts of their God-fearing parents to keep them on the straight and narrow path, away from worldly temptations. The only actual memory from the crossing that has come down to me, via Marie Anderson, is that of poor Oscar being sick over the rail while his father held his head. He was doubtless not the only one.

At length Long Island hove into sight, the pilot boat pulled alongside, and the ship sailed into New York harbor, landing its passengers at the immigrant receiving station at Castle Garden, on the Battery in Manhattan. If Gothenburg and Liverpool were impressive to these country folk, the great metropolis of New York was surely overwhelming. But we may assume that Sven Svensson was eager to press on to his final destination and to proceed with the business of finding land to settle on before the onset of winter. The family would therefore have taken the Pennsylvania Railroad out to Chicago, a journey of some four to five days, during which we may picture them alternately staring out the window at the strange landscape of their new homeland and quizzing each other on English words and phrases from one of the numerous guidebooks for Swedish emigrants available at that time.

It is not unlikely that they may have had the chance to visit with old friends, earlier emigrants from their home region, in

Chicago, for the city had early established its primacy as the Swedish center of the United States. Here as in New York, the arriving immigrants were likely to be set upon by "runners" and sharpers of all kinds, mostly, it is sad to relate, of their own nationality, seeking by various shady expedients to relieve unsuspecting "greenhorns" of their hard-earned savings. We may assume that Sven was adequately forewarned of such snares and kept a tight grip on the family exchequer. It is likely too, that the Svensson and Nilsson families were met in Chicago by Sophia and Victor Nelson, and perhaps by Ludvig or Sven Fredrik as well, who would then have accompanied them on the train to their destination, Altona, Illinois. They probably arrived there by late July—at the height of the midwestern summer—close to an even month after leaving Djursdala.

Altona, in Knox County some twelve miles northeast of Galesburg, consisted at that time of not much more than a general store, a blacksmith and wagon shop, doubtless a saloon, one or two simple wooden churches, and the small station of the Chicago, Quincy, and Burlington Railroad with its attendant water tower, straggling along its dusty, unpaved main street. It was here, however, that Victor's sister and brother-in-law, Emma Christina and Gustaf Johnson, were established since 1862 and here, too, Victor and Sophia were living since coming over in 1866. Significantly, most of Altona's local enterprises belonged to two brothers from Djursdala, who had been among the first three Swedes to settle in the vicinity in 1850. Their success had in turn attracted numerous others from their home region, as well as disaffected former members of the Erik-Janssonist sect from its communalistic colony at Bishop Hill some ten miles to the north, originally from Hälsingland and adjoining parts of north-central Sweden.[5] These circumstances make clear why Altona was the Svenssons' immediate goal in America: here they were surely able to stay with the Nelsons, the Johnsons, or with old friends from home while preparing for their next move.

Standing at the edge of Altona in 1973, looking out over the cornfields, I could not but wonder how all of this must have looked to the newly arrived family. To Sara Maria, worn out by travel, the summer heat, and the cares of her numerous brood, and with little Lovisa still at her breast, these strange new surroundings must have seemed frighteningly crude and primitive. She must have known her moments of despair and overpowering homesickness for all she had left behind her. The children were doubtless keyed-up and excited by this new world of novelty and adventure, yet inwardly bewildered by the flatness of the countryside and the absence of lake or forest somewhere within sight. For Sven the broad fields of ripening corn and the richness of the heavy loam under his boots must have outweighed all else. We picture the family being taken around the area by their hosts to call on various old friends and neighbors now established in modest prosperity in white clapboard farmhouses. We would also like to imagine, while we are at it, an excursion to the Erik Janssonists' Bishop Hill colony, with its impressive brick buildings along tree-shaded streets and its spreading farmlands.

Sven doubtless took every opportunity to inform himself about conditions in the new land and in particular about the best areas for settlement farther west. This last was a matter of lively discussion among the Swedes in Knox and neighboring counties at this time, for the available farmland in the area was now taken up and large numbers were beginning to move west, mainly into Iowa, in search of new land. The register of Altona's Swedish Lutheran Church tells this story clearly enough. During the 1860s its membership increased rapidly to its all-time high but by the following decade the general exodus to the west brought about its equally rapid decline.[6]

After some three months in Altona, Sven and his elder sons left for Iowa in search of land. The latter evidently included at this point Ludvig and John, as well as son-in-law Victor Nelson: Sven Fredrik meanwhile went to Paxton, Illinois, to attend the Augustana Lutheran Seminary there. Sven and his party must have traveled from Altona on the Burlington Railroad, which passed close by the New Sweden settlement in southeastern Iowa. We can imagine his reunion, at the Lockridge or

Fairfield station, with his father-in-law, the old America-farer Jonas Öhrn, who was surely full of sage advice, particularly when it came to selecting and acquiring land.

Continuing to Ottumwa—where they could have met Peter and Christina Anderson from Munterville—the land-seekers could then go on by rail to Des Moines, or some distance beyond, thereafter by wagon over the prairie. They stopped at Swede Bend (now Stratford), an old Swedish settlement in Boone County, then established themselves a few miles further north at West Dayton while they scouted for land immediately to the west.

The area around West Dayton (now simply called Dayton) in southeastern Webster County received its earliest settlers, including a family from Kisa in Östergötland, shortly before 1850, but remained the edge of settlement until the later 1860s, except for the isolated U.S. cavalry post at Fort Dodge (originally Fort Clark) some distance to the northwest, established in 1849 for protection against hostile Indians. Sven and his sons arrived just as Swedes from the older settlements in Illinois, including many from Altona, were beginning to take up land beyond West Dayton, in Lost Grove Township, named appropriately enough, for the only clump of trees within fifteen miles.[7]

The widow of Pastor C. J. Malmberg in West Dayton later recalled their first visit, by horse and wagon, to the Lost Grove area in 1868. They were looking for the Civil War veteran J. P. Liljegren's place, where her husband was to hold a church service.

> He had settled by a little creek some six miles further out than anyone else on that great grassy desert which lay between West Dayton and the present Gowrie. When we had gone six miles on the other side of West Dayton we could see nothing but the sky and a sea of grass. Mile after mile we drove, scanning the horizon. Not so much as a bird crossed overhead. Not an animal of any kind did we see—except for big snakes which lay here and there sunning themselves. When we finally caught sight of Liljegren, the pastor called out, "You have moved much too far out, Jonas!" But Liljegren

was of another mind. "Too far?" said he, "No, not at all. We will soon have a congregation here and then we will call Pastor Malmberg out to us." It did not take long before the pastor became convinced that his friend Liljegren had a broad view of the future. One house after the other was built in all directions around and about. Parents, brothers and sisters, cousins, and many others bought land and built their homes in this beautiful and rich area. Within two years the railroad came in and the station at Gowrie began to be visible only a few miles away.[8]

Sven quickly found what he was looking for. Government land was surveyed into townships consisting of thirty-six sections of 640 acres, usually divided into quarter sections of 180 acres for homesteading and sale. To encourage railroad construction, the U.S. government had granted extensive public lands to railroad companies, generally alternate sections along the right of way; by selling these lands at attractive prices to settlers, the railroads could recoup the costs of construction and at the same time build up future business by bringing population and economic activity into their areas. Lost Grove Township was railroad land belonging to the Chicago and Northwestern Line. Two sections of every township, Numbers 16 and 36, were meanwhile designated by law as school land, the sale of which was to pay for the establishment of local educational facilities. Before the end of 1867, Sven Svensson purchased the entire Section 16, 640 acres, at a price of $2.50 per acre or $1,600 in all. The transaction was closed at the courthouse in Fort Dodge.[9] By the end of the year too, it appears that Sara Maria and the younger children moved from Altona to West Dayton. Oscar Svenson later recalled making the last part of this trek by prairie schooner, some of the way together with another family.[10]

John Svenson would later relate about these early days: "The first time I saw Lost Grove was in the fall of 1867. With my father and brothers, and brother-in-law, Victor A. [*sic*] Nelson, we arrived in Dayton, Iowa. While there we saw an advertisement of land for sale in section 16, Lost Grove. Finding the land desirable, we invested and in 1868 we broke prairie with a five-yoke ox team. We built a shanty, 12' x 12', which furnished us a home. This cot was furnished with four beds, table, and kitchen stove, besides other household goods too numerous to mention. The only object we could see was the house of Mr. Jonas Liljegren, then in the process of erection. John August Danielson also stayed with us and broke prairie on his farm with a three-yoke ox team and a three-horse team."[11]

Farming was not easy during the early years. The terrain in Lost Grove Township is gently rolling and much of the low-lying ground was wet and boggy with numerous sloughs and ponds, providing the habitat for an abundance of fish and wild-fowl. For lack of natural drainage a good part of the ground could not be tilled before the turn of the century, when tile drain pipes were laid down on a considerable scale, an enterprise in which John and Oscar Svenson were much involved, recalling the similar efforts of their aging father back at Bullebo in the 1850s. The settlers meanwhile cultivated the higher ground, which was ample enough. Harvests were rich on the deep prairie loam and despite the rigors of the climate never failed.[12]

By 1869 Sven was meanwhile able to put up a frame house with lumber hauled close to forty miles by wagon from Boonesboro (now Boone), around which he planted shade trees brought from the bottomlands of the Des Moines River, some twelve miles to the east.[13] Sara Maria and the younger children were now able to move out onto the farm. The old house was to stand until the first years of this century. My father recalled hearing that Sven used to stuff the key holes with cotton during the winter; Marie Anderson remembers the old house as so drafty that you could smell the coal smoke inside when trains would pass on the Chicago and Northwestern track that was constructed a short distance north of the houselot a year or two later. We can imagine what it must have been like when the icy northwester swept down off the plains in winter or during the relentless, humid heat of summer. I was thus not surprised to hear my Aunt Margit recall that she had heard Sara Maria never ceased to grieve for the comfortable home she had left in Sweden.

Religious services were held occasionally on the Liljegren and J. A. Danielson places by Pastor Malmberg from West Dayton and an outbuilding on Danielson's farm served as Lost Grove Township's first school, which the younger Svenson children attended. With the building of the Des Moines and Fort Dodge Railroad, the town of Gowrie came into existence in late 1870, about two miles northwest of the Svenson place, on land where Oscar Svenson could later recall having gathered prairie hay. On 21 January 1871 twenty-one persons gathered to organize a Swedish Lutheran congregation. Sven Svenson, who now spelled his surname with one s in the "American" fashion, kept the minutes of the meeting and forwarded the group's application for admission to the Augustana Lutheran Synod. His son John was one of the five churchwardens elected at this organizational meeting. M. C. Ranseen was brought in to serve as the community's first pastor.[14]

The settlement grew and the prairie blossomed. It would not be long before Webster County would have a larger Swedish population than any other in the state, except only for Polk County with the city of Des Moines. Gowrie, with well over half its inhabitants of Swedish derivation, became one of the principal centers of the largest area of continuous Swedish settlement in Iowa, extending through Boone and Webster Counties.[15] And Iowa, along with the neighboring states of Illinois and Minnesota, lay at the heart of Swedish America.

7

Forerunners

Like many of the early immigrants, Sven Svenson was a man ahead of his time in his native place. In Djursdala he had sought to bring about changes that threatened the old ways of doing things and put him on strained terms with his more traditionally minded neighbors. Arriving on the Iowa prairie at the age of fifty, however, he still remained very much a peasant patriarch at heart.

My father once told me in a half-facetious manner that old Sven had wanted to build himself a kind of "empire" on the frontier, surrounding his home farm with those of his children. This is the way Dad would have heard it from his father, Ernest, who had little use for such an idea. Yet it was no doubt true enough and this should hardly be surprising. We can well imagine Sven's ideal to have been a godly, Swedish community in a rich and bountiful land—a kind of idealized Djursdala— where he and Sara Maria could live out their days amid their numerous children and grandchildren, as his own father, Sven Arvidsson of Karsnäs, had done before him. Sven purchased an entire section of land—640 acres—at the outset. Before long he would arrange for certain of his children to take over parts of it.

I have found two photographs of Sven Svenson, taken in the 1870s and 1880s. The first, from "Leisenring's New Photographic and Fine Arts Gallery" in Fort Dodge, shows Sven and Sara Maria, together with daughter Frida, then evidently eight to ten years old, which would date the picture around 1872–74. The second, of Sven alone and by a Denver photographer, is dated 1889 on the back. The figures are well dressed, revealing a decent prosperity. Sven's expression and bearing are those of a man apparently confident of his affairs in both this world and the next, a paterfamilias accustomed to authority and respect, while Sara Maria, strong-featured and clear-eyed, is his worthy matriarch.

But this was America, not Småland: the old, stable relationships of the Swedish countryside could not be transplanted intact to a new continent in the throes of rapid development. One by one Sven's and Sara Maria's children made their way out into this great new world of opportunity and peril until only three remained in and around Lost Grove. It is thus time to turn from the parents to the children, beginning with those who preceded them to the new land.

We have seen that the first to leave was the second son, Ludvig Daniel, who came to America in June 1864. It seems certain that his father had helped with the expenses of his voyage and that Ludvig came out as his family's advance scout, a common enough arrangement during the emigration. Some nine months after his arrival the twenty-year-old Ludvig *Swanson*—as his name is recorded—enlisted on 10 March 1865 for one year's service in Company C, Forty-third Illinois Volunteer Infantry Regiment in Peoria, Illinois, and after training at Camp Butler, Illinois, was sent down to Arkansas.[1]

Ludvig's place of residence at the time of his enlistment is given as Lynn—now Lynn Center—four miles west of Andover, Henry County, Illinois. We have already seen that the first recorded emigrant from Södra Vi parish was Samuel Jönsson from Örsåsa, who departed in 1846. After various misadventures in the East he arrived in Andover in 1848 and later settled near Orion, four miles north of Lynn. The first two emigrant families from Djursdala parish, those of Nils Magnus Nilsson and Pehr Svensson—the latter unrelated to our family but from Bjorkesnäs, adjoining Bullebo—sailed over together on the same ship in 1849 and both settled around Andover. Pehr is remembered, incidentally, for having constructed the first wheeled vehicle to be made in Henry County, an ungainly oxcart in which he and his sons could often be seen driving to church. In 1850 Gustaf Peter Hoflund and his family from Djursdala came to Andover and thereafter located near Orion. Many followed from these and nearby parishes.[2] Thus Ludvig undoubtedly had friends to come to in the Andover-Orion area in Henry County.

He arrived in a nation at war. Since the beginning of the Civil War in the spring of 1861 the Scandinavians in the Midwest had responded enthusiastically to President Lincoln's call to arms. Out of some twenty-five hundred Swedes fit for military service in Illinois during the course of the hostilities, more than half, or some thirteen hundred men, volunteered for the Union forces, a higher proportion than that of the population of the state as a whole. Company C of the Forty-third Illinois Volunteers was an all-Swedish unit which had first been raised in Galesburg, Knox County, in April 1861 and included many men from neighboring Henry County. Since then it had given a good account of itself in combat in Tennessee, Mississippi, and Arkansas. From the spring of 1864 it was on garrison duty at Little Rock.[3]

Ludvig was one of the last recruits to join his company. The end of the war was now expected momentarily and the Confederacy in fact capitulated at Appomattox only a month later, on 9 April 1865. My Aunt Margit remembers hearing that the war ended just when her uncle was ready for action. Ludvig had surely been anxious to join before it was too late.

Abraham Lincoln and the Republican party had no more stalwart a following than among the Swedes of the Midwest. This was perhaps especially true in the president's home state of Illinois, where Pastor Tufve Nilsson Hasselquist of Galesburg, since his arrival from Sweden in 1852 the dominating figure of Swedish Lutheranism in America, brought to bear his own powerful influence and that of the first regular Swedish-American newspaper, *Hemlandet, det Gamla och det Nya*, which he himself had founded in 1855, for the preservation of the Union, the freeing of the slaves, and—the Republican party's liberal land policy.[4] The Scandinavians, among others, were rewarded with the passage of the Homestead Act in 1862. Many young Scandinavians immigrated to America during the later war years and joined the Union forces in anticipation of enlistment bonuses— Ludvig received "33⅓" dollars—and generous veterans' benefits, above all quick citizenship and free homestead land. Ludvig, it seems clear, was one of them. He served for eight months, until his unit was demobilized in Little Rock, Arkansas, in November 1865.

Thereafter little more is heard of him. He presumably returned to Illinois and may have been living in or around Altona, in Knox County, when his elder brother, Sven Fredrik, arrived there in 1866 and the rest of the family the following year. He was surely with his father, his brother John, and brother-in-law Victor Nelson when they went out to Iowa looking for land in 1867. He was one of eight U.S. citizens who petitioned for the legal incorporation of Lost Grove Township, which took place in October 1870, and he thereupon became its first supervisor for road construction, while Victor Nelson served on its first school board. Ludvig, however, did not long remain there. By 1876 he was living in Des Moines.[5]

We have seen that Sven and Sara Maria Svenson's third child and eldest daughter, Maria Sophia, was married to Frans Viktor Nilsson of Solberga, Skede parish, in March 1866, thus being the only one of their children to marry in Sweden. Already in June the same year the young couple left for America, together with Maria Sophia's oldest brother, Sven Fredrik.[6]

Victor Nelson, as he now called himself, was already an "old American," having been over before, in 1860–64. In 1866 he and his bride came to Altona, where his sister and brother-in-law, the Johnsons, were living. It was here that Sophie, as she was now called, gave birth to their first child, Joseph, in February 1867.[7] Sven and Sara Maria Svenson's first grandchild thus awaited their arrival in America.

Thereafter, Victor accompanied Sven Svenson and his sons, John and apparently Ludvig, to Iowa to look for land. Sophie and their child probably moved together with Sara Maria and the younger Svenson children to West Dayton, Iowa, later that same year and stayed there until it was possible to move out to

Lost Grove. Two years later, in 1869, Victor and Sophie purchased the southwest quarter of Sven's section of land and built their home there, which is still standing. In the meantime more children were born to them.

In 1870 Sven Svenson donated a hilltop, close to the middle of his section, to be used as a cemetery by the Lost Grove settlers. The oldest gravestone, on the crown of the hill, is inscribed with the names of six children born to Sophie and Victor Nelson between 1870 and 1888, all of whom died between the ages of one month and four years. It tells us much about their parents' lives during those years, indeed much about life on the prairie frontier a century ago. Besides their first child, Joseph, four others would reach maturity: George, Frank, Elmer, and Ellen.

In 1860 representatives of the Swedish and Norwegian Lutheran congregations in the Midwest met at the little Norwegian settlement of Jefferson Prairie, near Clinton, Wisconsin, to establish their own Augustana Lutheran Synod, from which the Norwegians would later secede to form their own body in 1870. The Reverend T. N. Hasselquist of Galesburg was elected president, a post he was to hold for the next decade.

The same year Pastor Esbjörn, formerly of Andover, set about organizing the Augustana Seminary for the training of Scandinavian candidates for the ministry, at the Immanuel Lutheran Church in Chicago. In 1863 the seminary was moved to Paxton, Illinois, some 110 miles south of Chicago on the Illinois Central Line, where Reverend Hasselquist assumed the rectorship. The following year preparatory and college departments were added and in 1865–66 the total student body at Paxton amounted to forty-four. The need for pastors was great within the newly formed synod, which raised the hopes of poor students of peasant background in Sweden who saw little chance for ordination and appointment within the state church, among them many of the young men at Pastor A. P. Ahlberg's school for lay preachers and missionaries at Kristdala, later at Ahlsborg, in Småland. To them the little seminary on the Illinois prairie seemed the answer to their prayers.[8]

In August 1866 Pastor Hasselquist received a letter from Sven

Fredrik Westerdal, Sven Svenson's eldest son, who had just arrived from Sweden together with his sister and brother-in-law, Sophie and Victor Nelson. Young Westerdal sought admission to the seminary in Paxton and inquired about financial aid, without which he would have to borrow money before the term began in September. He pointed out that he had taught for three terms at Pastor Ahlberg's school in Sweden and could if need be help with instruction in certain subjects in Paxton. He had left Ahlberg's school because of poor health, which for a time had seemed to stand in the way of his entering the church. "But praise the Lord, it is now better, so that I hope with redoubled strength to take up again what I have neglected." He was now living with a certain Sannquist in Altona, although he was just then visiting his old school friend, Pastor A. W. Dahlsten in Galesburg.[9]

Dahlsten wrote separately to Hasselquist the same day, vouching for "Brother Westerdal," whom he had known in Stockholm. "A humble and devoted disposition makes him dear to me—I hope with all my heart that he will be accepted." Although his health was delicate, Dahlsten did not consider it a serious obstacle. He added that Sven Fredrik had taught "several languages" at Ahlberg's school and that he had not received a letter of recommendation from there because Pastor Ahlberg "did not want to let him go because of the instruction," although he otherwise had nothing against him. Dahlsten concluded by pointing out that Westerdal was very poor and in debt for his journey over.[10]

Rector Hasselquist in Paxton was wary. While the need for pastors was great in the new land, he was determined to maintain high standards within the ministry. He was meanwhile increasingly importuned by young hopefuls from Sweden with only the faintest prospects for success. He therefore wrote to Sven Fredrik:

God's peace! I received your letter yesterday. Regarding acceptance to the Seminary with support, I must admit that some difficulty evidently arises since you do not have with you or have not had sent any recommendation from Pastor

Ahlberg. He has sent here and recommended reliable young men and has even warned us against those he could not recommend. It would look badly if we accepted someone from his school without his recommendation. This is to cast no shadow over Brother Westerdal, whom I know of already from the brothers who have come to us from Ahlsborg. But I believe we must have a letter from Pastor Ahlberg first. There is meanwhile nothing to prevent you from studying here if you have means to support yourself for at least one term, during which all obstacles may be cleared up. With that reservation, you are most welcome, together with Brother Sannquist. Greet him and his dear wife.[11]

To Pastor Dahlsten he wrote confidentially that his concern was increased by "a brother" at Paxton who "had seen" Westerdal and expressed some reservations concerning both his health and his character. "May the Lord help us in our choice of students and send to us such as are and will remain faithful and believers."[12]

Thus commenced under unpromising auspices a hard and troubled pilgrimage in the new land. Sven Fredrik spent only a short time in Paxton in the fall of 1866. Already in March 1867 the lay preacher in New Sweden, Iowa, Håkan Olson, wrote to Hasselquist that Brother Westerdal had been teaching school there during the winter and was well regarded. Hasselquist's reply, however, showed concern over Westerdal's indecision and lack of direction, and indicated that he was still not considered a regular student at Paxton. The following month Sven Fredrik wrote to Hasselquist from Knoxville, Illinois, where he was supporting himself by copying music and had a chance to teach school in nearby Galesburg. He confessed that he had gone through a time of doubt and uncertainty, that he had been "a sheep gone astray." But through God's grace he had come to the full recognition of his sins. He thus hoped to return to the seminary and enclosed a small donation toward its support.[13]

What had happened? Both ill health and lack of funds may have cut short Sven Fredrik's studies. In New Sweden, meanwhile, he would have been reunited with his grandfather, Jonas

Öhrn, a staunch Methodist. Although he had taught school to the satisfaction of the Lutheran congregation there, may the unspecified transgressions of which he spoke in his letter to Hasselquist not have arisen, at least in part, from Methodist doctrines that were anathemas to Lutheran orthodoxy? We can no more than speculate.

Sven Fredrik was evidently back in the seminary again in 1867–68. In February 1868 the Mississippi Conference of the synod was prepared to employ him as a catechist in Burlington, Iowa. The following month, Håkan Olson in New Sweden reported that his congregation was considering whether to call Westerdal as its regular pastor, if he could be ordained by 1869, and asked Hasselquist's advice, particularly since some parishioners feared that his health might not be up to the rigors he would have to face. What these could be were indicated in the same letter, when Olson described how both he and his horse had often come close to being carried away in the spring and autumn floods while making the rounds of his far-flung parish.[14]

This, however, was the sticking point. Hasselquist replied to Olson that Westerdal's "sickly body had made his spirit depressed and gloomy" to the point that the seminary had felt compelled to advise him to suspend his studies, without a year or two more of which there could be no question of his ordination. "We should seek to give W. work and bread," he wrote, "but he probably cannot hope to become a minister."[15]

Poor Sven Fredrik thereafter disappears from view for over a year. Perhaps he went home to his family, by now established at Lost Grove. In the summer of 1869 Pastor Eric Norelius accepted his third call to serve at Vasa, Minnesota, where in 1855 he had founded one of the first Swedish Lutheran congregations in what was to become the most "Swedish" state in the union.

As his assistant Norelius now selected Westerdal. For the next nine months Sven Fredrik made the rounds of the western expanses of the parish although sometimes hindered by the state of his health. In February 1870 he wrote to Hasselquist requesting ordination so that he might accept a call from the neighboring Cannon Falls and Cannon River congregations to the west. His health was much improved, he reported, his views more certain than when he had last been in Paxton, and his resolve to serve the Lord renewed. Hasselquist's opinion of his capabilities had improved and he now wrote Norelius that he could in good conscience recommend Westerdal for ordination, since he had already acquired "no little knowledge" in Sweden and had spent some time at the Paxton seminary. Yet at the annual synodical meeting in Andover, Illinois, that year, Sven Fredrik was denied ordination on grounds of his poor health.[16]

When he next wrote to Hasselquist over a year later, in April 1871, he was serving the Cannon River and Cannon Falls congregations as a catechist and had been sent by the Minnesota Conference to preach to Swedish settlers in several other places in the state. That year he was formally graduated from the seminary in Paxton and in August he married Anna Lovisa Johnson.[17]

There followed a long silence, which was at length explained when Sven Fredrik next wrote Hasselquist from Holmes City, Minnesota, in the fall of 1873: he had twice suffered acute sunstroke while on a preaching tour in 1871. This "scourge and chastisement of the Lord" had left him incapacitated for two and a half years, throughout the first of which he was confined to his bed. The Lord had seen fit "to strike me with His rod so that I learned that grace and terror were my daily fare along with my tears." Sven Fredrik must have anguished in the thought that his God had forsaken him, only to seek solace in the reflection that He tries most severely those He loves the most. He was now able to move about with the aid of a crutch, had taught Swedish for a few weeks, and was preparing some candidates for confirmation in Holmes City.[18]

Sven Fredrik had meanwhile received a call from the congregation in Gowrie, Iowa, where his family was settled, and he implored Hasselquist finally to set his mind at rest as to whether he might ever hope to enter the clerical order. Hasselquist could only reply that the matter must be decided by the Minnesota

Conference, which was best acquainted with the circumstances of the case. In the meantime he counseled prayer.[19]

The circumstances were evidently such as to cause further delays. In 1874 Sven Fredrik taught Sunday school for a time in Gowrie. It was not until 27 June 1875, nine years after he had first sought admission to the Augustana Seminary in Paxton, that Sven Fredrik Westerdal was at last ordained, at the synodical meeting in Vasa, Minnesota. It must have been the happiest day of his life. He had been serving at the time as assistant to the pastor in Andover, Illinois, where his first child, Sven David, was born in June that year. He now received his first congregations in Henderson Grove and Wataga, near Galesburg in Knox County, Illinois.[20] Sven Fredrik's tribulations were over, at least for the present.

8

A Window into the Past

The year 1875 was of particular importance not only in the life
of Pastor Westerdal but for our narrative as a whole, for it was
then that his brother John went out to California. During his
absence there, various members of his family and friends wrote
numerous letters to him, which he preserved, thus providing
us with a far clearer picture of the affairs of the Svenson family
between late 1875 and the end of 1876 than we have for any
other period, before or after.

The time was fortuitous for our purposes, for it was one of
generational change and readjustment within the family. The
strains and conflicts which resulted were intensified by hard
times in the United States and particularly in agriculture, following the financial crisis of 1873. Before we open this unique
window into the past, however, we should consider the recipient of the letters, Johan Theodor—now John T. Svenson—
Sven's and Sara Maria's fourth child and the eldest of those who
came with them across the Atlantic in 1867.

John was hardheaded and resourceful. He must have learned
English quickly and well during the first pioneering years in
Lost Grove, for already in 1874–75 he was able to spend a year
at Iowa Agricultural College (now Iowa State University) in
Ames and secure a teaching certificate. This officially qualified
him to teach in the little one-room schoolhouse which is still
standing as an outbuilding on the old August Danielson farm,
about a mile southeast of the Svenson farmstead, where his
younger brothers and sisters went as pupils, although he had
apparently done some teaching there already. It seems that he

did some farming too, on his father's land, much of which was still uncultivated.[1]

But John was not yet ready to settle down. He needed a stake if he were to get a proper start in life. He was interested in things mechanical and had a hankering to see more of the world. Besides, times were hard for farmers. In 1875 he therefore packed his valise and headed west. He found employment in the maintenance shops of the Central Pacific Railroad in Sacramento, California, where he may also have spent some time working in 1873–74. Letters now began to arrive from home.

They show that Sven and Sara Maria were feeling their years. Since that summer, especially, both were ailing. Sara Maria was burdened with the whole household since Matilda was in Andover, Illinois, and Sven was so poorly off that Victor Nelson feared he might have *lungsot*, or consumption—evidently a faulty diagnosis, since he would live another thirty-three years! They thus felt that the time had come to turn the farm over to their children.

What they had in mind at this point was for Ludvig, John, and Oscar—or perhaps the latter two—to farm "in company," that is, cooperatively, sharing the profits of labor and investment as agreed upon between themselves, their parents, and brothers and sisters. The arrangement may not have been uncommon within farming families in the American Midwest at the time. It is in any event reminiscent of traditional provisions for the transfer of family farms in the old Swedish peasant society, in which the old parents lived on *undantag* in their own separate house on the farmstead, supported according to contract by their children.

That such an arrangement would be unwieldly at best was clear enough to John, and as he wrote to Oscar, he did not feel like working for others any more. But what made it impossible was a keen rivalry between Ludvig and John. At some earlier time they had received assurances from their parents that they could each buy half of the northwest quarter. By the end of 1875 John was prepared to offer nine dollars an acre for his share. Sven replied that ten dollars was the lowest they could go; to accept less would, he feared, cause dissatisfaction among the other members of the family. He must have had Ludvig especially in mind and may indeed have proposed the cooperative farming scheme largely as an attempt to avert conflict.

Ludvig had been following a somewhat itinerant existence in recent years, practicing an unspecified trade. At the turn of the year he was working in Des Moines. He did not fail to react strongly to John's offer. Although he had no real interest in even a single foot of his father's land, he frankly informed Sven in February 1876, he was prepared to buy up John's promised eighty acres at fifteen dollars apiece, as long as he could get his own eighty "for what we discussed," to keep John from acquiring them. At the price John offered, the sale of the eighty acres would leave only a meager return, once Sven's debts were paid off, and John would "come home and become your guardian." Ludvig claimed not to be concerned with his own profit but only "for you and the interests of my younger brothers and sisters." He proposed to build a new and larger house next to the old one. Unfortunately for his ambitious plans, he was short of ready cash and he was not earning in Des Moines as well as he had hoped. In the meantime he urged his father to rent out as much land as possible.

Ludvig surely meant well. He was doubtless warmly attached to his parents and perhaps he really hoped to hold most of the family together on or near the old place. But he was fanciful, suspicious, and quixotic; Victor Nelson said that "with Ludvig Daniel you could never figure out what he had in mind." He was also improvident, as shown by his later, constant appeals for financial help and utter poverty at the end of his life.

John was nothing if not practical. His grandson, Clifford Swenson, claims that he was always basically more attracted to mechanics than to farming. The situation at Lost Grove compelled him to face a difficult decision, which he may in part have been seeking to avoid by going to California. He was under a certain moral obligation to buy the offered eighty acres from his parents and knew that they were counting on him, especially in view of Ludvig's undependability. Yet he liked what he was now doing and his new-found independence. It is not unlikely that he bid low on his parents' eighty acres in the hope that his offer would be rejected, releasing him from any further obligation. At the same time he dropped hints that he was thinking of going to Oregon to seek land there. All of which caused Sven and Sara Maria, as well as his younger brothers and sisters, much anxiety.[2]

There was another reason for John's quandary, namely Carolina Larson, daughter of a Swedish family which had moved to the Gowrie area from Andover, Illinois, where Carolina had been born and grew up. It would seem that John had left for California just at the time when it was expected he should declare his intentions and indeed his indecision in this matter may have been a reason for his going. Now John wrote, separately and confidentially, to several of his brothers and sisters, and to his brother-in-law Victor, seeking their advice regarding both Carrie Larson and the question of the land purchase. While all insisted he must do as he saw fit, they favored Carrie, "a real good girl," as Ernest called her, and stressed how much they all missed him. They generally felt too, that John was really committed to buy the eighty acres. In any case they all hoped he would return to Lost Grove, although Victor felt that even if he bought land there, he might well keep his job in Sacramento until times improved.[3]

By March 1876 the purchase of the eighty acres was definitely off; John considered ten dollars an acre more than he was willing to pay, rather to the chagrin of Victor, who had done his best to mediate the deal. Ludvig now undertook to buy John's intended eighty at fifteen dollars an acre together with his own eighty at ten dollars an acre. By May Sven had rented out forty acres and built a cabin for the renter on the northeast quarter. Victor nonetheless offered to look for other land in the vicinity and urged John to make up his mind quickly so that he could cultivate it for him before summer. In June Matilda wrote John that she had seen some land that was being considered for him.[4]

John was meanwhile a bashful suitor. After a long mutual silence, Carrie Larson wrote to him in March from Marshalltown, Iowa, where she had taken a job in a household, assuring him she had not forgotten him and that indeed "I maybe think more about you than you do about me." He had said when he left for California that he would come home after a year and she now reminded him that the time was approaching. In May she was delighted by a letter he had sent her, together with his portrait, and replied that she loved him truly and was glad that he was "not going back on what we talked about." [5]

In July, John at last came home, to the delight of his family and not least, of Carrie, but he was ill and remained in poor health throughout the fall. Carrie's mother seemed opposed to their marriage, perhaps fearing that the young couple might leave the area. In his discouragement John considered going back out to California. He was encouraged in this thought by a Swede he had known there, one N. Johnson, who wrote from Belleville, Nevada, that there was no point in trying to farm in the Midwest, where, as he had heard, the grasshoppers had eaten everything, and that as for the girl, he could find another just as good without fuss or nonsense, "for when one goes, another stands there in her place. So let the girl go her way and come back to Sacramento." Another crony, E. Nystrom, writing from Sacramento in his best English, proffered the advice that if his girl did not love him, "dont grief about that neither, the world are full of girls and the are more anchous to yet married than the men." From Marshalltown Carrie wrote in despair, urging John to see her before he might leave and reassuring him about her mother. In Henderson Grove, Illinois, Brother Westerdal obtained medical advice and assured John that marriage would improve his health. In the end he stayed in Lost Grove and by the later fall was teaching school there again. [6]

In February 1877 John and Carolina Larson were married, beginning their long and happy life together. Carrie was determined not to leave her family, so any further thoughts of California or Oregon were now laid to rest. They bought eighty acres of unbroken prairie in Section 18, about a mile and a half west of the old Svenson place and an equal distance south of Gowrie, to which they added another forty acres in 1895. Here they built the house where their grandson, Clifford Swenson, is still living. Their son, Carl Theodore—whom I met there in 1957 —was born in March 1878. A daughter, Sara, born in 1881, lived for only a few months.[7]

The letters John received during 1875–76 meanwhile tell us much about the rest of the family at this time. Pastor Westerdal, now in tolerably good health, wrote of family and church affairs in his parishes in Henderson Grove and Wataga, Illinois. In 1876 the newly ordained minister attended the annual meeting of the Augustana Lutheran Synod in that eastern bastion of Swedish America, Jamestown, New York, where he witnessed the sobering spectacle of the defrocking of two brother clergymen for "grievous sins and ungodly behavior," amid "many tears and prayers to the Lord."[8]

Sister Matilda, or "Tilda," as she was called in the family, was in Andover, Illinois, ostensibly to learn to play the organ from Pastor Erland Carlsson's daughter but principally to get over a heartbreak caused by one John Main in Gowrie, whom John Svenson in California feared might also be a rival for Carolina's attentions. Tilda adopted Brother Westerdal's surname and much of his pietism, repeatedly urging John to turn to Jesus e're it were too late. In May Sophie Nelson became so ill that Tilda, much against her own inclinations, was called home to Lost Grove to see her sister one last time in life. Sophie gradually recovered but her parents seemed more tired and ailing than Tilda had expected. "I do not believe they will get very old," she wrote John, "they have to work too hard in their old age." Thus, although she got her beloved parlor organ from Andover, Tilda could not return there herself. The family needed her too much at home. Poor Tilda. She had her dreams. In January she began to wish she could go back to school, "for here it has become so much the fashion to be able to do something." At twenty-four, however, she feared she might already be too old to learn.[9]

Arvid Fritjof, who now called himself Irving F. Westerdal, was attending Augustana College, then in its first year following its move in 1875 from Paxton to Rock Island, Illinois. Poor health caused him to drop out during the winter and seek medical help in Chicago, after which he taught "Swedish school" in Sven Fredrik's Wataga parish during the summer of 1876. In October 1877 he was working at some unspecified job in Green Mountain, apparently in Iowa. Irving was a restless and fearful soul. His father wrote to John in December 1875 that Irving had "changed his views since you last saw him" and had written, begging his parents for their forgiveness "for all the times he had been in error." "May God give him grace that he may continue," Sven added. If this suggests some questioning of the faith, his adoption of the name Westerdal may indicate something of his repentence, for during the winter Irving's ill health filled his mind with obsessive thoughts. "It is on the lungs," he wrote mournfully in his solemn Swedish English, "I feel the death accationally." A doctor in Chicago soon thereafter diagnosed his problem as a "liver complaint." In the meantime he ruminated much on divine grace and redemption. For a time Irving changed his name to Westerdale, then eventually shortened—and anglicized—it to West. This too is indicative, for Irving, the sixth child in his family, was evidently the first to feel uncomfortable about his Swedish background and to rebel against it. His path led him farther and farther away from Iowa and from his origins.[10]

Ernest wrote numerous letters to John, filled with light-hearted, irreverent banter which shows the particular closeness between them. It was intended that Ernest should follow in Irving's footsteps, and to this end he left the nest at the age of sixteen to spend the winter with Brother Westerdal and family in Henderson Grove, Illinois, there to prepare himself for college with his brother's help in such subjects as Latin, German, Swedish grammar, and history. Pastor Westerdal and his parents were anxious to put Ernest into the godly and Swedish Augustana College. Ernest himself was tempted to follow the example of his more worldly brother John and go to Iowa Agricultural College in Ames, with its secular and American atmosphere. He was in any case avid for knowledge. "I wish I had an Edycation," he wrote to John that spring, "but I dont have

it and so I must studdy so as to get it." He gave some indica-
tion of his future development when he complained of the local
youths, who instead of discussing "Education, Civilization, The
Nations, &c.," could talk of nothing but "cows, calfs, and a
funny pup, &c."

From April through June Ernest taught Swedish school at his
brother's church in Henderson Grove, striving to impart some
correct knowledge of the mother tongue to "the worst children
for making a racket I have ever seen." He visited Rock Island
and Orion, where he had friends named Hammer—possibly
relatives of his grandfather Öhrn's last wife—but for some
reason apparently not nearby Altona, where he had spent his
first months in America nine years earlier. In July Ernest moved
to Andover, having collected only twenty dollars of the eighty-
five dollars due him for three month's teaching, and worked for
a farmer for his room and board while boneheading Latin grammar under the tutelage of the local pastor's son, Carl A. Swensson, who later made a name for himself as president of Bethany
College in Lindsborg, Kansas. That fall he started out at Augustana College, where he was especially intrigued by a course in
shorthand. By Christmas he had fallen ill and he seems to have
dropped out for the remainder of the academic year. He is listed
in the Augustana College catalog for 1877–78 as a freshman
and in the following year as a sophomore.[11]

Oscar, who came between Irving and Ernest in age, had by
the end of 1876 clearly become the "home son"—the *hemmason*
in the old Swedish tradition—whose responsibility it had become to cultivate the family farm and to look after his aging
parents. For years to come he would labor there, patiently and
without recompense. At Christmas, 1875, he was touchingly
grateful for a suit of clothes, finer, he claimed, than any in Lost
Grove, even if the trousers were a bit large, which John had
passed on to him from California. Emil and Frida were still
children, too young yet to go out into the world.[12]

Certain impressions emerge from this pile of century-old letters. The first is that of the burden of ill health, which this
family—like countless others—had to bear under the harsh con-

ditions of the prairie frontier. The summer heat and winter cold were both much more severe than they were accustomed to from southern Sweden and the old frame houses gave only limited shelter from either. Standing water in a multitude of bogs and sloughs bred mosquitoes and produced an oppressive humidity during much of the year. Medical science was as rough and ready as the frontier itself and could offer few specific remedies. It seems little wonder that every member of the family, except Oscar, Victor, and perhaps one or two of the younger children, was afflicted by more or less serious bouts of illness— generally described in terms of "pains in the breast" or "dry coughs"—that Sophie lay at death's door in May, or that she had lost six infant children during the preceding five years. Given such conditions, one can only admire all the more what they were able to achieve for themselves and their descendants.

The letters from Sven, Victor, and Oscar give details about the Svenson and Nelson farms: about Sven's six teams of horses, the breaking of thirty more acres of land, the planting of wheat and of more corn than before, the raising and sale of hogs. Underlying all this is the constant anxiety of the times over low and fluctuating prices for farm produce and lack of ready money. On top of this, 1875 had been a wet year with a poor harvest while in 1876 the Midwest was visited with one of its periodic plagues of grasshoppers. Things were so bad, Victor wrote in January 1876, that he was considering quitting farming if they did not improve within the next year. Victor had suffered a serious loss a week earlier when his hay supply was burned up in the field by a prairie fire, but it is cheering to note that the loss was made good by his father-in-law, Sven, and thirteen other neighbors, each of whom contributed a cartload of hay.

One reason why John received as many letters as he did during this period was that his brothers and sisters were in constant need of ready cash at a time when he alone had a steady and decent income. He was constantly lending or simply giving money—$5.00, $10.00, up to $40.00 or more at a time—to Sven Fredrik, Tilda, Irving, Ernest, and to Victor, who also borrowed seed wheat from him. Notations on the back of an envelope from February 1876 show that already at that time Victor owed John $344.00 for cash loans plus another $100.00 for wheat, while his father owed him $138.00 and Tilda $80.00. The picture is one of meager resources, niggling debts, pinched prospects. Ernest, for example, departed for Illinois with a grand total of $7.41 from his parents, to repay a debt to Brother Westerdal, and "not a cent for me." He was so shabby, he complained, in Oscar's patched and threadbare old trousers, Ludvig's old overcoat, and his own battered boots that he dared not show himself at "meeting" in the church. A loan of $10.00 from John permitted him at length to outfit himself, quite handsomely he thought, at one-third off at a bankruptcy sale in Galesburg.

It is notable that the letters almost never mention Sweden or the old home. In April Ernest mentioned that he was boarding in Galesburg with a certain Fredrik Larson and added, "He is from Södra Vi, he said that he often used to hold Pappa's horses when he was in to see Grandfather, and so on." How gladly would I know what that "so on" included! Following the Augustana Synod meeting in Jamestown, New York, Sven Fredrik wrote from the small Swedish settlement of Sugar Grove, Pennsylvania, "I am now visiting Carl Johan Svensson (Söderholm) from Karsnäs, Södra Vi parish." [13] Nothing more. If, amid their everyday cares, their thoughts sometimes returned to their native place, their letters give no expression of this. Perhaps the emotional wrench of leaving behind all that had been near and dear, and of coming out to the desolate, windswept sea of grass on the Iowa prairie had been so great that they wanted to be reminded of it as little as possible and thus drew a discreet veil over the past. This reluctance may have been strengthened in some of them by secret misgivings, brought on by the hard times of the mid-1870s, over the wisdom of their ever having left Sweden. For the older ones there was always the consolation of religion, of eventually reaching the pilgrim's true home with God. But for some of the younger ones, who ultimately came to question the old orthodoxy, there remained to the ends of their lives a certain restlessness, an unfulfilled yearning.

The letters illuminate, finally, how the family was adapting to the American environment. As we have seen, Irving and Ernest were showing signs of rebellion by 1876, upon leaving the family home and community; in time Emil and Frida would reveal something of the same inner conflict.

This process of cultural reorientation was, however, nowhere more evident than in the use of language. Sven Svenson, although he made use of some of the more common Swedish-Americanisms connected with farming and land measurement, always used his native tongue, having little need for English in and around Gowrie, where even "American" businessmen reputedly picked up some rudimentary Swedish. Marie Anderson claims he never learned enough English to form a proper sentence. Sara Maria knew surely even less. Neither, incidentally, was much given to writing. By November 1876 Ernest had heard nothing from his father since leaving home eleven months earlier. When Sophie seemed near death in May, Tilda received the longest letter her mother had ever written to her—a whole page.

Pastor Westerdal, while he naturally knew English, wrote a formal, at times flowery, literary Swedish in a copperplate hand. Ludvig's English, as preserved in a single letter from 1906, was faulty but serviceable. The six-year-younger John learned the new language well and spoke it with scarcely a trace of an accent. Both continued to write good, grammatical Swedish. Victor Nelson's letters are in a rich mélange of Småland dialect and anglicisms which would gladden the heart of scholars of Swedish-American syntax; although he had first come to America before any of the others, he confessed in January 1876 that he was no "quick fellow when it came to reading and translating English." Oscar, who likewise had little opportunity for schooling, wrote a labored and more or less phonetic Swedish, as did Tilda and the American-born Carolina Larson. The letters from Ernest, and especially from Irving, in 1875–76 are usually written in a careful, but uncertain and quirky, English that reveals their determined struggle to master the new language— taught in school but not used at home—and thus to make their successful passage into the mainstream of American life. Oscar and Ernest, at least, and doubtless Irving and the younger children as well, would eventually lose any trace of a Swedish accent, although they would always continue to use Swedish on occasion. Surviving fragments from Emil and Frida in this period are written in a childish American Swedish.

Acculturation was taking its natural course. Yet the Swedish language would remain long-lived among Sven's and Sara Maria's descendants in the New World. A century after these letters were written to John there are grandchildren and great-grandchildren living in this country who can still speak the old tongue.

9

The Family Go Their Ways

Since coming to America before the rest of the family, Sven Fredrik and, for the most part, Ludvig had been on their own, while Sophie had her own home and family. During 1875–76, the "younger family"—as Clifford Swenson calls them—began to leave home: John, Tilda, Irving, and Ernest. After the end of 1876 there is little documentation on the Svenson family, at least until the 1890s. There is enough, however, to follow its members as they went their various ways in life.

It may be remembered that Sven Fredrik—or "Fredrik," as his family now called him—had received a call from the Swedish Lutheran congregation in Gowrie in 1873 but had been unable to accept it since he was not yet ordained. The congregation, which Sven Svenson had helped to found in 1871, continued to struggle on as it had before, generally sharing a pastor with West Dayton and meeting alternately in the Gowrie Township school and in August Danielson's schoolhouse in Lost Grove for services generally conducted by elected deacons.[1] In April 1876 Fredrik received a second call from Gowrie but declined it, perhaps in part because he had not yet served a year in his congregations in Henderson Grove and Wataga, but partly too, it might seem, because the salary offered was too scanty. A third call came in July 1877 and this time Fredrik accepted, doubtless encouraged by the congregation's decision a few months earlier to build its own church and parsonage.[2]

The construction of these buildings was the most noteworthy accomplishment of Fredrik's years in Gowrie. At times he was called upon to preach in other communities without pastors of their own and during 1878 he was given leave to raise money for the new Swedish Lutheran Church in Fort Dodge. As was frequently the case, the Gowrie parish was divided into *rotar*, or wards, and under Pastor Westerdal the practice of *husförhör*, or annual pastoral visitations to each family in the parish, was introduced, both on the model of the Swedish state church. In March 1880 we find Fredrick writing to Rector Hasselquist at Augustana College in Rock Island, asking if his alma mater could provide a "Christian-minded young man, who might exercise a salutory influence on the children," to teach both in the English-language public school and in a three-month Swedish school in Lost Grove, at thirty dollars a month. The new church was dedicated in 1882, rewarding an impressive fund-raising effort by the local Swedish Lutherans. The congregation in Andover, Illinois, showed the strength of its ties to what was largely its daughter colony to the west with a contribution toward the building of the Gowrie church.[3]

Fredrick could well take satisfaction in the fruit of his labors. While in Gowrie, Lovisa bore their second child, Ester Elisabeth, in October 1880. Another daughter, Lydia, died in infancy and was buried in Lost Grove Cemetery. It may have been in connection with the birth of this child that Lovisa herself died in November 1881, leaving the thirty-nine-year-old Fredrick a widower with two small children to look after. Eleven months later he was remarried, to Mathilda Teresia Björkman, in October 1882.[4]

In January 1883 Fredrick Westerdal resigned as pastor of the Gowrie congregation and left the community later that year.[5] Why he did so is not clear. Six years in the same congregation was about normal for Augustana Lutheran pastors at the time, yet he could doubtless have remained longer if he had wished. He probably had already received the call he would next accept, yet it seems doubtful that Calumet, the rough and ready copper-mining town in Michigan's Upper Peninsula where he now went, could have offered many amenities to tempt him and his family to leave Gowrie. Perhaps the loss of his first wife and infant daughter made him anxious for a change of scene. Or his new wife, who came from a comfortable and cultivated middle-class family in Malmö, may not have felt at home in Gowrie or around her country in-laws. There could, however, have been other causes. Early rural immigrant communities often brought to the affairs of their religious congregations hostilities and rivalries that would later find outlet in local and national politics. The archives of the various denominations are filled with the echoes of bitter contentions, often over seemingly trivial matters. It is not unlikely that Fredrick found himself caught up in some unrecorded discord in Gowrie, which would have been all the more painful to him since his own family would have been involved. Clifford Swenson remembers hearing it said that Pastor Westerdal was "*too* religious," that he was a real "hellfire and damnation" preacher. He had born a heavy cross for his faith and his uncompromising views may have put him at odds with those in his congregation who preferred a broader and easier road to salvation. Maybe he felt that now the congregation in Gowrie was well under way there was a greater need for his ministry among the "greenhorn" immigrant miners in northern Michigan.

Fredrick served in Calumet for two years, during which time Mathilda gave birth to a son, Fredrick Samuel, in August 1883. The family would thereafter never remain long in any one place. Mathilda died already in September 1885 and Fredrick and his three children moved on. In 1885–87 he served in Westby, near Irvine, Pennsylvania, and in 1887 married Mathilda's younger sister, Ida Carolina. It was said in their family that this match was Mathilda's dying wish for the sake of the children. In 1887–88 they were in Houtzdale, Pennsylvania. During the next two years, 1888–89, Fredrick served in the unique and isolated New Sweden settlement in northern Maine, founded in 1870 by William Widgery Thomas, Jr., a former American consul general and later ambassador to Sweden, and a noted Suecophile. Thereafter, in 1890–91, the family was in Port Henry, on Lake Champlain in northern New York State. During a part of his time in the East, most likely the last year or two, Fredrick served the New York Conference of the Church as a missionary pastor in various localities.[6]

About these years in Fredrick's life we know only the barest outline. About Ludvig, however, we know even less. In applications for a veteran's pension, submitted in 1907 and 1914, he claimed to have lived, since mustering out of the army in November 1865, in Arkansas—probably for only a short time immediately following his discharge—in Illinois for seven years, thereafter in Colorado and Idaho. Curiously, he failed to mention Iowa, where as we have seen he lived, evidently from 1867 until 1876, if not later. Most of his seven years in Illinois must thus have come in the later 1870s and early 1880s. According to family tradition he went out to Colorado to prospect for gold and this same activity may also have taken him to Idaho.

By the later 1880s he was in Denver. On 22 September 1891, he wrote to John on stationary bearing the letterhead, "L. D. Swainson, Dealer in Wall Paper, Paints, Varnisheds, etc., etc., 620 17th Street, Denver, Colorado." In view of the expected sale of his part of the family farm in Lost Grove, he hoped John could obtain two thousand dollars "in clear hard cash" for him, after deducting the mortgage and what he owed his father. Times were now worse in Denver than he had ever seen them and his business was not making expenses. It is unclear whether he was able to get any of his money out of the farm before the whole nation was overwhelmed by the Panic of 1893, the worst of the century. This seems to have done in his business in Denver, for in 1894 he moved to Cripple Creek, Colorado. His occupation there is given as "farmer" in his 1907 pension application. From at least 1900 on Ludvig was in poor health and constant need of help, and both Oscar and Ernest, if not others in the family, sent him what they could.[7]

As he had already considered doing during the hard times in 1876, Victor Nelson left farming in the later 1880s and moved into Gowrie, where he opened Nelson and Son's Hardware Store. Characteristically, Gowrie's business community was almost exclusively Anglo-Saxon during its early years. It was only after the first decade and a half of the town's existence that Swedish farmers and their sons from the surrounding countryside began trying their hands at town occupations. Both Victor and his son Joe were members of the town's first band, between 1883 and 1890, and were later joined by George. In 1891 the Gowrie post office was moved into Nelson's hardware store and Victor was made postmaster by political appointment.[8]

The Nelsons' daughter, Ellen, recalled that her mother, Sophie, was the community's first tooth-puller. After administering a stiff shot of whisky, she would apply a device called an elevator and tighten the screw until "something had to give." After Dr. A. O. Peterson opened his office in Gowrie, Sophie limited her practice to the old settlers, "who were tough and could take it."[9]

The Nelson boys were engaged in a variety of enterprises during the following years. In September 1892 Joe and Frank bought the *Gowrie News*. Only two months thereafter a fire burned down Nelson's Hardware and neighboring businesses. Victor's and Sophie's grandson, Crayton M. Watkins, Jr., claims it was generally understood to be a case of arson. Prohibition on the sale of alcohol through local option was an explosive issue in Iowa at the time. Gowrie was a dry town and through the *Gowrie News* Joe Nelson made himself known as the most outspoken of the local "drys." Irish "wets" were suspected of burning down Nelson's Hardware, although this could not be proven. As elsewhere throughout the Midwest antipathy ran high between the staunchly Protestant Scandinavians and the fervently Catholic Irish. Prohibition was frequently a sore point of conflict between them. Even if the Irish were not involved in this instance, it shows how profoundly the Swedes tended to mistrust them. Whether or not there was any connection, Joe and Frank sold the newspaper in April 1893. Nelson's Hardware was already that year back in business in new quarters. It was sold in 1902. Five years later Victor Nelson retired as postmaster.[10]

After some time back on the family farm, Tilda went to St. Paul, Minnesota, to work as a domestic. Here she met and married Dr. C. E. Lundgren, a man evidently some years older than herself, sometime around 1879.[11]

The Augustana College catalog shows that Irving was back in 1878–79, when he was enrolled in the third class of the preparatory department. He did not finish there, however, but drifted east, where he long worked for the Pennsylvania and Erie Railroad, painting and decorating coaches. At the end of his life, if not earlier, he was living in Brooklyn.[12]

Oscar remained on the family farm until he was thirty-two years old. From 1888 to 1893, he was in Omaha, where he worked for two chinaware importing firms in succession. In the latter year he married Maria Charlotta Lofstedt and returned to Lost Grove to cultivate the old farm.[13]

In 1893 drainage of sloughs and wetlands through the laying down of permanent, underground tiling began in Webster County. Both Oscar and John Svenson played prominent parts in this useful work and John took a short course in surveying to prepare himself more effectively for the task. It was through such efforts that this main obstacle to cultivation was overcome, making the county one of the richest farming areas in the Midwest and a far healthier environment for its inhabitants. Before this, many Swedes from the area had already moved on to new Swedish settlements in southwestern Iowa, Nebraska, and Kansas, largely because of humidity and ill health.[14]

Ernest's illness at the end of 1876 apparently forced him to drop out of the preparatory program at Augustana College for the time being, but the college catalogs show that he was back as a freshman in 1877–78 and as a sophomore in 1878–79. He is described as a good student with a great eagerness to learn at this time, but ill health again interrupted his studies, so that he had to return to schoolteaching to support himself. In a fragment of a later letter to his niece, Ellen Nelson, he recalled, "at the time I was struggling to get through college—taught school at $24, $30, $35 [a month] without board and one winter I got $45 as principal of Imogene School." (Imogene is in Fremont County, in Iowa's southwestern corner.) In the meantime he was drawn to a medical career. When he was able to take up his education again, it was at Amity College, a small institution of learning in College Springs, Iowa, last listed in the *World Almanac* in 1912. Here Ernest graduated with the "Baccalaureate of Science" and went on to study medicine both in Iowa and Nebraska. In 1885 he was awarded his M.D. degree by the University of Nebraska Medical School in Omaha, where he now hung out his shingle at 117 North Sixteenth Street.[15]

The only letters I have discovered from Ernest's Omaha years are two brief notes in 1888 to his "dear little nephew," Theodore, in Gowrie, consisting of the kind of good-natured banter that had filled much of his correspondence with the boy's father, John, a dozen years earlier. As he was now in fortunate circumstances himself, he undertook to help certain of his brothers and sisters, much as Sven Fredrik and John had done earlier. It was while he was in Omaha that Oscar came there to work. About the same time Emil arrived to study pharmacology at Creighton University, then Frida, who had been living for a time with sister Tilda and her husband in St. Paul, Minnesota, and who now most likely found work as a domestic.[16]

In 1889 a Swedish Ladies' Quartette from Stockholm came to Omaha to perform. Ernest, who attended their concert, was captivated by the first soprano, Jenny Norelius. Afterward he was asked to escort her to a party at the home of some friends of his who were related to friends of hers in Stockholm. As she later told it, she descended into the lobby of her hotel in the old type of cage elevator and when she caught sight of Ernest, waiting below and looking up at her, their eyes met and it was love at first sight. Very soon thereafter they became engaged.

Jenny Christina Charlotta Norelius was born in Länninge, Bollnäs parish, Hälsingland, in northern Sweden, the daughter of a *häradsskrivare* or district recorder, in 1863. After her father died in 1875, her mother moved with her four children, first to Uppsala, then to Stockholm, where Jenny studied singing at the Royal Conservatory of Music in 1882–85. As she was venturesome and enterprising, she undoubtedly welcomed a chance to see something of the Great Land in the West. Of the Swedish Ladies' Quartette which sailed for America in 1889, all four of

its members would remain in the new land, including the second soprano, Jenny's younger sister, Vilhelmina or "Mina." [17]
Jenny departed Omaha with the quartet for points west. When the tour was over she returned to Stockholm to get her mother's consent to marry. Ernest went to Chicago for clinical study of nose, throat, and ear ailments. When Jenny returned they were married by a justice of the peace in Kenosha, Wisconsin, in January 1890 and in July they moved out to Portland, Oregon. [18]

It is not known just why they made this move but we may venture some informed guesses. Ernest was, as would become increasingly evident, a restless, searching dreamer. His favorite brother, John, had been fascinated by Oregon in his time and perhaps Jenny on her tour had been attracted there by a nature so similar to her beloved native land. The well-known Swedish-American author and journalist, Ernst Skarstedt, then living in Portland, wrote a quite detailed biographical sketch of Dr. E. O. Svenson in his *Oregon och Washington*, published in 1890—upon which most of what I have to say about him in this chapter is based—from information provided by one of Ernest's "oldest friends and one of those most knowledgeable about his past." [19] This good friend, whoever he might have been, may perhaps have encouraged Ernest to come to Oregon, as he in his turn would draw after him both Emil and Frida. All of them exemplify the westward migration of Swedes in America, both from the older settlements in the Midwest and directly from Sweden, by the end of the nineteenth century.

Dr. and Mrs. Svenson established themselves in a house in the Piedmont district in northeast Portland. It was here that their first child, my father, Sven Hildor Barton, was born in November 1892. Emil was there at the time and Frida was among those present in the christening photograph from the following March, as was the portrait of old Sven Svenson on the wall. Both Emil and Frida helped the young family celebrate Christmas in 1894. [20] Jenny gave birth to their second child, my aunt, Margit, in August 1896.

Ernest did well for himself at first. The redoubtable Skarstedt, who would later express the fear that the medical doctors were becoming a new priesthood, was prepared to assert in late 1890 that "E. O. Svenson is among the few physicians for whom we dare to predict a brilliant future."[21] Ernest was able to set Emil up in business in a pharmacy, in which he himself was a silent partner.[22] Frida most likely worked as a domestic, at least part of the time, then drifted east to seek new opportunities and experiences.

In 1887, meanwhile, a niece of Sven Svenson's, Mathilda Charlotta, daughter of his brother Anders Svensson Kindgren and grandmother of Karin Augustinson, emigrated from Rumskulla parish, Småland, to Rock Island, Illinois, with her husband, Samuel August Samuelsson, five sons, and two daughters—the whole family, that is, except Karin's father, who had just completed his training as a church organist. They evidently had little or no contact with the Svensons in Iowa. In 1924 Karin visited her grandparents in Rock Island, a year before they both died. But until she began her genealogical research in 1967 she was unaware that she had any other relatives in the United States.[23]

10

The Passing of an Era

The reader who has been keeping track may well wonder by this time what had become of Sven and Sara Maria's youngest child, Lovisa, or Louisa, as her name was spelled in America. She was only a half a year old, a babe in her mother's arms, when the family came to the new land in 1867. After that I have found out nothing about her except that she was the first in her family to depart this life, in February 1875, at the age of nine. Old Sven remembered her tenderly as his "little girl."[1] Louisa left no more trace of her brief existence than the record of her birth and the hazy memory of her death. She was laid to rest in Lost Grove's hilltop graveyard, overlooking her family's fields and pastures.

Shortly before Christmas, 1887, Sven and Maria left the old farm in Lost Grove they had labored on for the past twenty years and moved into Gowrie, to live with Sophie and Victor Nelson, who had now established themselves there. Shortly thereafter Sara Maria became ill and took to her bed. "During her illness," her obituary states, "she maintained repeatedly that she left herself entirely in God's hands and accepted His will." On 18 August 1888 she died at the age of sixty-five and was buried beside Louisa in Lost Grove Cemetery.[2]

In 1891 Fredrick Westerdal, his third wife Ida, and his three children returned to Sweden to stay. Again we have no explanation and must resort to conjecture. Fredrick's path had been strewn with thorns ever since he had come to America; certainly Ernest, and probably others in his family, felt he had been treated badly by his synod. His frequent movements since leaving the Gowrie congregation in early 1883 would seem to suggest problems of adjustment. Already in 1886 and 1887 he obtained the first of several testimonials from conference and synodical authorities in America which he submitted to the Härnösand diocese of the state church in support of his application for accreditation as a pastor, upon his arrival in Sweden. It seems not unlikely that Ida, whom he married in 1887, was not happy in America and longed to return to her homeland. In any event, Fredrick and his family now joined the estimated 18 percent of the Swedish immigrants to the United States who eventually remigrated to the old country between 1875 and 1925.

While waiting for the Härnösand diocese to act on his application, Sven Fredrik—it is proper that we now revert to the original Swedish form of his name—served for some months as an unofficial assistant to the pastor in Atlingbo parish on the island of Gotland. On 27 April 1892 he was accepted into the clergy of the state church by the Härnösand cathedral chapter, whose diocese included all of the northernmost part of Sweden, provided he once again became a Swedish subject and acquire a sufficient knowledge of the Finnish language to serve in the border parishes in Lapland.[3] In September he passed his theological examination before the cathedral chapter and was appointed adjunct pastor in Karungi, Karl Gustaf parish. He was assistant pastor in Pajala in 1893, vice chaplain in Korpilombolo in 1894, adjunct pastor in Karungi, 1895. In November 1898 he was moved south to somewhat more civilized surroundings when he was made assistant pastor in Anundsjö parish in Ångermanland. Here he died in September 1900, worn out at the age of fifty-eight.[4]

It may seem that Sven Fredrik, after his hard and dedicated labors in America, received but scant consideration from the state church in his native land. Yet such was the common fate of those Swedish-American pastors who returned to Sweden. The ecclesiastical establishment continued to look askance at the upstart, independent Augustana Lutheran Church, with its evangelical zeal, moral puritanism, and lack of liturgical splendor or of an authoritarian hierarchy. Ernest considered his eldest brother a man of simple faith.[5] In a way he seems not really of this world. After Sven Fredrik's death, his family moved to Karlshamn in southern Sweden. The eldest son, Sven David, went to Uppsala University, where he was a member of Gotland's "Nation," or student fraternity, and took the degree of *filosofie kandidat* in 1902. There is a letter from him to his Uncle John in Gowrie, written in February 1903 from Karsnäs, Södra Vi parish, where he was staying with relatives. He complains of ill health, thanks John for sending him twenty-five dollars and urges that "Old Grandfather" Sven, who had been kind to him before, be persuaded to send him more money to allow him to continue his studies, especially as he did not get along with his stepmother, who gave him no help.[6] Marie Anderson recalls that her father, Oscar, would often send money to Sven David, at some sacrifice to his own family. Ester Elisabeth, who had been born in Gowrie, became a schoolteacher in Ryd, Småland, and Marie remembers how she and her father went to Fort Dodge to find children's books in English to send her for her pupils. But all contact with the younger Westerdals was lost after a few years and only Karin Augustinson's painstaking inquiries through various pastors' offices in Sweden were recently able to uncover something of their later lives.

Sven Fredrik's widow, Ida, died in Karlshamn in 1909. Ester Elisabeth moved to Sundsvall in northern Sweden in 1910, where she taught school until her retirement. Sven David remained a kind of perpetual student in Uppsala and was looked after by his devoted sister during his last years. He died in 1951 and is buried in the plot for Gotland's Nation in Uppsala's Academic Cemetery, directly across the street—as chance would have it—from the home of a latter-day relative, the retired chief librarian of the University Library, Gert Hornwall. The second Westerdal son, Fredrik Samuel, was working as a masseur in Karlskrona in 1905 and married the same year. A son, Martin Fredrik, was born in July, and in November 1905 all three left for America, with some financial help from Oscar Svenson in Lost Grove. We have found no trace of what happened to them thereafter. In February 1970, Ester Elisabeth Westerdal died in Sundsvall at the age of ninety.[7]

After leaving the farm at the end of 1887 and Sara Maria's death the following summer, old Sven lived with Sophie and Victor Nelson in Gowrie for eleven years. The Nelsons' daughter, Ellen, remembered her grandfather from her childhood and "no one ever loved anyone as much as I loved him."[8] Oscar returned from Omaha to cultivate the family farm and married Maria in 1893. Four years later, in 1897, Sven returned to the old place to live with them. Oscar's and Maria's daughter Marie Anderson, born in 1895, remembers him as a frail and slender old man, about five feet ten inches in height. Since coming to Lost Grove at the age of fifty his health had never been robust and he often felt out of sorts. He used to dig roots and gather bark and herbs on the prairie, from which he brewed teas to cure his ills, and he was skillful at budding and grafting fruit trees. He could sit by the hour, telling stories with "Grampa Schill" and "Grampa Kullgren" in the front room while little Marie listened from behind the door. "He could paint word pictures so vividly," she recalls, "that you could almost see them."

During his last years, Marie feels that he was more concerned with the life to come than with this life on earth. Each morning Sven would sit in his captain's chair in the parlor and conduct family devotions, beginning with the old hymn: "Du klara sol går åter upp/ För mig och fader kär [Each day the sun goes up again/ For me and Father dear]." He was full of pious verses and would admonish his little granddaughter: "Himmelens glädje och helvetets pina låt aldrig gå ur tankarna dina [May the joys of heaven and the torments of hell never leave thy thoughts]."[9]

During his last years the old man became increasingly frail and helpless, imposing a heavy burden upon Oscar and especially Maria. Sadly enough, this gave rise to renewed dissension within the family. At the time he came to live with Oscar and his family, Sven made over to them seventy-six acres of land in return for maintaining him for the rest of his life, retaining one hundred sixty acres in his name. Oscar and Maria considered this only just compensation, especially since Oscar had stayed home and worked without wages on the family farm until he was over thirty, while his brothers were furthering their education and getting ahead in life. In 1902 conflict arose when Sophie, John, and Ernest felt that Oscar stood to profit unduly from this agreement, at the expense of his brothers' and sisters' rightful inheritance, since the value of the land had increased considerably over what it had been appraised at when the agreement had first been entered into. Both sides clung stubbornly to their viewpoints, embittering relations between them for long years to come. Ernest returned for some months from Oregon to confer with Sophie, Victor, and John. The result was a lawsuit in March 1903 over their father's legal competence, which was successfully upheld by Oscar and Maria. Sven, the object of this contention, wondered "why they could not leave an old man alone." Half of his remaining quarter section had to be sold to pay the legal fees.[10]

In 1904–5 Oscar built a new house, where Marie Anderson still lives, next to the old one, which not long after was torn down. The new house was roomier, more comfortable, and warmer in winter. Here old Sven lived out his last years. In July 1907 they took him, as they often did, up to Lost Grove Cemetery to visit Sara Maria's grave. "The next time I come this way," he said, "I will come to sleep with Mother."

He declined rapidly during the months that followed and on 1 August 1908 he died. Marie remembers that he lay praying rather indistinctly in his room upstairs. Around dawn she was sent, barefoot, to fetch a neighbor because Grampa was "bad." Oscar came in from the barn to sit with him. Marie was there when he breathed his last. Just before he smiled peacefully. Marie believes that at that moment he saw his Lord. He was laid to rest beside Sara Maria on the hilltop amid the land he had first broken forty years before.[11]

Sven Svenson lived to the age of ninety-one years, four months, and two days. What had he not seen and experienced during his lifetime, since his birth in 1817 on faraway Karsnäs farm in Södra Vi parish! He had been brought up in a traditional peasant culture, then in the very flower of its development, yet he had played his part in the new trends which by the time of his death would largely break up the old way of life and create a Sweden very different from that in which he had grown up. He sought a new life for himself and his family in the American Midwest and had labored mightily to transform the prairie frontier into the settled and prosperous farming area it had now become. He was already a young man when the Swedish emigration to America, properly speaking, began. By the time of his death over a million of his countrymen—an estimated one out of every five Swedes—were living in North America, and within less than two decades, while most of his children were still living, the great migration came to an end.

Out in Cripple Creek, Colorado, where he had been living since 1894, Ludvig was in failing health from at least 1900. In December of that year he applied to Washington for a veteran's invalid pension, attesting that he was a bachelor and wholly incapable of supporting himself due to "lung trouble," catarrh, rheumatism, kidney problems, poor eyesight, and "general debility." It was around this time that he last visited Lost Grove, where he suffered so badly from his respiratory condition that he had to sleep sitting up in a chair and returned to Colorado after only two days. The matter of his pension dragged inconclusively for the next several years, apparently in part because he had enlisted in the Union army in 1865 under the name *Swanson* but now called himself *Swainson*. Oscar, Ernest, and doubtless others in his family sent him such money as they could spare. In 1906 Ludvig again applied to Washington, this time mentioning heart trouble and partial deafness among his disabilities. He was then boarding in a house on a back alley in Cripple Creek. It would seem that he was finally awarded a pension of twelve dollars per month in 1907. Nothing is thereafter heard from him until April 1914, when he wrote to the Bureau of Pensions in Washington from the Colorado Soldiers' and Sailors' Home in Monte Vista, requesting an increase in his pension since he had just reached the age of seventy. A memorandum from the home shows that he died already the following month. He had evidently been out of touch with his family for years. My Gowrie relatives believed that he had died around 1904 and had been buried in a potter's field. He was no doubt laid to rest in the veterans' cemetery at Monte Vista.[12]

In time Tilda also largely disappeared from view, although under happier circumstances. There is a jovial Christmas and New Year's letter from St. Paul, Minnesota, written all in verse, from her husband, Dr. Lundgren, to his parents-in-law in Lost Grove in January 1883. This reveals that by now they had a little daughter, whose name is not mentioned but who was just beginning to say her first words; she was surely the "Cousin Ruth" my Aunt Margit remembered hearing about. The letter also shows that Frida Svenson, here referred to as "Elfrida," was living with the Lundgrens in St. Paul, where she was helping with the household while going to school. In the mid-1880s the Lundgrens moved to Brooklyn, New York; Frida in an undated letter, apparently from around 1900 when she was in the East, gives their address there. Tilda is understood to have eventually moved to Washington, D.C., perhaps after becoming widowed, where she worked for the Government Printing Office and in time became a supervisor in the Postage Stamp Division. In her youth she had longed to "do something," and we may imagine her as contented in her responsible position. It is not clear when she died or where she is buried. Her daughter, Ruth Lundgren, married a man called Richard Roseberry; while they could not recall the details, my father and aunt used to say that one of their cousins had married a relative of the English earls of Rosebery. The couple had three children—Edwin, Richard, and Ruth Francis—who are shown in photographs from their home in Washington, D.C., probably from around 1910 or thereafter. I have, however, been unable to learn what later became of them.[13]

Irving was also in the East, largely out of contact with his family. He died, a bachelor, in New York City—probably Brooklyn—in 1921. He left a bequest of something over a thousand dollars to each of his nephews and nieces, which helped my father in college and his sister Margit to leave the main post office in Seattle, where she had been working, and study in San Francisco for a career as a fashion artist.[14]

Emil was the youngest son in his family and seems to have been spoiled accordingly. He came to Omaha to go to college while Ernest and Oscar were there. When Ernest married and moved to Oregon, Emil followed along. Ernest set him up in Portland as a pharmacist, until the partner in the business absconded with the funds in the Panic of 1893. Around 1898 he went back to Gowrie and spent the summer with Oscar and his family but was impatient and demanding. Sometime thereafter he was working in a drugstore in a little town of Nehalem on the Oregon coast. My father seemed to recall that he was even mayor there for a while, although this involved nothing more than jailing a drunk Indian one time. My Aunt Margit heard that he had suffered disappointment in love and remembers him as irritable with children. He never married. At that time narcotics, such as opium or cocaine, were not restricted nor was the danger of using them very well understood. Emil eventually acquired an addiction of some kind which surely undermined his health. He returned to Portland and together with his cousin, George Nelson from Fort Dodge, set up "Svenson's Ladder Works." By 1917 his health gave out. Ernest did his best to care for him, but to no avail. He died that year at the age of fifty-six, with Ernest and his niece Margit at his bedside in a cheap hotel.[15]

Frida, who likewise never married, had a particularly adventurous life. Sometime around the turn of the century she left Oregon for the east, where she found work as a lady's maid and companion in wealthy families. There are notes from her in the years following, from fashionable communities in Connecticut and Massachusetts. In one undated note, on letterhead stationery saved from the Hotel Bristol in Naples, she speaks of having traveled with her employers in Europe the previous winter, which she enjoyed immensely and hoped to repeat. Unfortunately she gives no details, although she enjoyed Paris the best. Gösta Karlsson in Djursdala says he has heard it said that a daughter of Sven Svenson once came back to the old parish to visit. If this is true, it was most likely Frida, on this or a subsequent trip. During this period she picked up some of the affectations of her genteel employers and called herself Miss Winnifred West, adopting the name of her brother Irving, with whom she must have then been in contact.

In 1914 she was back in the Northwest, working as a housekeeper for a family in Seattle. She now assumed Ernest's surname and called herself Miss Fred Barton. A note, jotted on the back of the menu for the captain's dinner aboard the S.S. *Victoria* in June 1916, next shows her on her way to Nome, Alaska. Upon arrival she found herself a job as cook in a mining camp near Bluff, five hours by boat from Nome, at one hundred dollars per month. She realized how surprised her family must be that she had come to Alaska and felt as though she were at the "end of the world." A year later, after the mine was sold, she found work in a hotel in Council, two days by boat from Nome and no "pleasure trip." Six weeks later the hotel closed down, but making her way overland back to Nome Frida was offered and took a job cooking for a small group of miners. She was at this point not sure she would stay in Alaska but felt she really had nowhere to return to. She sent John an article from the *Eagle Magazine* for August 1916, giving picturesque details about life on the Seward Peninsula.[16]

In April 1919 she wrote on the letterhead stationery of the Lavinia Wallace Young Mission for Eskimos in Nome, maintained by the Methodist church. Since the past November she had been working as a nurse, for the last ship into Nome that year had brought in the Spanish influenza, which carried away 185 Eskimos and 30 white people within three months: "My! The sights among the natives were terrible. Whole families were found dead in all manner of positions. In one house nine natives were picked up; their coffins had to be made according to the position they were in when they died, for they were frozen. It seems most of the young and healthy natives passed away, while the old, the consumptives, and the children were spared. . . . I forgot to tell you that this has been the coldest winter for a good many years. There were days when the thermometer registered 56 below zero and coal cost 36 dollars a ton." [17]

Although she herself got off with only a light touch of the flu, Frida must have worn herself out that winter. Yet she always used to say afterward that her Alaska years were the happiest of her life, since they had made her feel "important." By 1920 she was back in Seattle, working for a former employer from Alaska, but the next year she suffered a disabling stroke. She went to Fort Dodge and lived with Sophie until the older sister herself became ill. She thereafter spent some months living with Sophie's daughter Ellen and her husband in Gilmore City, Oscar and Maria on the old farm, and John and Carrie in Gowrie. Although she fascinated her younger relatives with her accounts of Europe and Alaska, and showed flashes of her former good humor, her stroke had left her gloomy, irritable, and hot-tempered. After a final row with John she was sent back out to the West Coast. At this point it seems that "an ex-soldier" somehow managed to make off with what remained of her savings. She was now totally dependent upon Ernest and Jenny, who arranged for a Mrs. Pullen in Gresham, Oregon, to take care of her. She died in Portland in 1925, aged sixty-two. [18]

When we come to Ernest, we have far more to go on and I find him of particular interest, not only because he was my grandfather but because he was a sensitive and articulate man, whose numerous letters from 1893 on give a remarkably revealing picture both of himself and of the inner conflicts experienced by many immigrants who arrived in America at an early age. His letters to John from Illinois in 1876 show him warmly attached to his family and background, yet at the same time show independence of spirit and the desire to make his own way in the world. His next preserved letters to John, from Oregon in the mid-1890s, reveal a stronger reaction to his origins.

The first of these, from February 1893, tells us something about the recipient and much about the writer. John had longed as a young man to acquire an education, Ernest wrote, had worked hard for one, and "condemned the selfishness of those who did not attend to the mental welfare of their children."

Now John's own son, Theodore, was fifteen years old and "if you want him to get the instincts of a gentleman 'tis time he was learning." Ernest thus offered to bring Theodore out to Oregon for two years at Bishop Scott's Academy, "the best school for boys on the Pacific slope," where he would receive the proper upbringing. "John," he continued,

> I left home 2 years too late to be a gentleman in the finer manners. I have attended banquets where I had to respond to toasts and I have felt the lack of that something which every early trained boy possesses. Now I do not mean a fop. God forgive me if I held such notions. I do not mean snobbishness—no, I mean a man such as God made him with the rough corners of habit worn off. John, two things will cause me to one day fill a mediocre man's grave: my name (foreign) and my lack of *early* training. Without either you should one day hear from me! Now, when my name suggests the alien, they look for the manners of the emigrant and behold, they need not wait long. Now, if this was neutralized my chances in life would be doubled, yes, quadrupled. . . . I hope you understand me. You had the energy to lift yourself above your neighbors, I had the same. . . . Our first duty is to improve our mental faculties—let the material wealth come as it can.[19]

It is all here: the ardent concern for "higher things," for the cultivation of the mind; the longing to rise above the "common herd"—as John himself used to put it—to be accepted into the social and cultural elite and to enjoy its amenities; yet at the same time the lofty unconcern with the crass pursuit of money. All these motifs would recur repeatedly thereafter.

The question of Ernest's surname brings into focus his problems of acculturation. In August 1876, he had written to John from Andover, Illinois, "Everyone insists that I must give up Svenson and take the name Westerdal, but I don't believe that, for I am not ashamed of my good old, tried and true, Swedish name, Svenson."[20] In part this would seem to show how he identified with his independent-minded brother, John Svenson, as opposed to the more pietistic Tilda and Irving, who adopted Pastor Westerdal's name.

The family story is, meanwhile, that when Ernest went to college, either in Illinois or Nebraska, there were so many named Svenson in the school that they agreed among themselves—or were encouraged by their rector—to adopt other names. This was not uncommon practice in schools in Sweden and a similar story was told of Sven Fredrik's adoption of the name Westerdal there before his immigration to America. As Ernest was interested in medicine and admired the Civil War nurse, Clara Barton, he chose her name. The change was, however, surely not official, for when he entered practice after 1885, his office letterhead was inscribed "Dr. E. O. Svenson, the only Swedish Regular Physician in Omaha, Neb." His marriage certificate from 1890 bears the name Svenson, although his children, born in 1892 and 1896, were apparently always called Barton. Yet in 1896, three years after the letter to John, cited above, his name is given on the letterhead of the Yamhill County, Oregon, Bryan election committee as "E. O. Svenson." He was still, during these years, evidently prepared to use either name, as might be convenient, and Svenson could attract Swedish patients and votes for the Democratic party. After 1900, however, he went over entirely to his new name.[21]

In the literature of the nineteenth century the physician often personifies the new, freethinking, scientific mentality, as opposed to the intellectual conservatism of the priest. By the 1890s Ernest, while still affectionately attached to his family and boyhood home, was in conscious reaction against his past. The economic crisis of 1893 deeply alarmed him and in 1896 he threw himself, heart and soul, into the Democratic party's campaign for the election of William Jennings Bryan, thereby breaking with the traditional Republicanism of the Swedish midwestern farmer.

Why, he asked rhetorically in January 1895, should his brother John have only four thousand dollars in debts to show for thirty years of hard and honest toil, while during the same years two thousand persons in the United State had become millionaires? "You did not get enough of a harvest to pay the interest on the money; for interest on money there are never any crop failures!"

The Republicans were to blame; "there has never been a more shameful political party since we came to America." Yet in their blindness millions of farmers continued to vote for them. The Democrats, under Grover Cleveland, were not much better. Ernest thus felt that the Populists, with their policy of free coinage of silver, were the only salvation for the suffering masses.[22]

During 1896, the election year, the so-called "silver" wing of the Democrats gained control of their party and co-opted both the Populists' program and their presidential candidate, William Jennings Bryan of Nebraska, the "boy orator of the Platte." Ernest threw himself enthusiastically into the Bryan campaign and by October was gratified to learn that both John and Oscar were "on the road to political wisdom," while Emil was "a Bryan Man Sure!" As an Oregon state committeeman, Ernest had a long talk with the Populist leader, Senator "Pitchfork Ben" Tillman, who read John's latest letter with satisfaction and commented, "When a man gets far enough to let go his prejudices he is all right—your brother cannot be fooled any longer." Although he looked forward to devoting himself after the election to "philosophical and scientific subjects," Ernest's heart was with the "plain people." "When . . . I shall be called before the Supreme Judge of the Universe to give an account of doings . . . I don't apprehend any questions about why I did not help Hanna, the bankers, the trusts, the monopolies, the syndicates and combines, even if they have now become known as the Republican party!" The defeat of Bryan by the Republican, William McKinley, was a bitter blow to Ernest and his friends. He remained, however, one of the stalwarts of the Democratic party in Portland for the rest of his life and in 1924 there seemed some possibility of his being offered a patronage job for his forty years' devotion to "The Cause."[23]

Most significantly, Ernest rebelled against his pietistic religious upbringing. In college he discovered the cultural heritage of the Western world and later, looking back, found his childhood years arid and deprived, intellectually and aesthetically. He claimed, for instance, that he never heard any "music"— other than hymns, that is—until a peddler once came to the farm and played "Steamboat Comin' 'round de Bend" on his mouth organ. In college he once sang the part of Mordacai in Mendelsohn's "Elijah" and he remained a music lover throughout his life.[24] He similarly discovered secular literature—American and European, including Swedish—art, physical science, the comforts and amenities of polite society.

At the same time he became sharply anticlerical, not least with respect to his own church. "Speak of the power of the Catholic clergy," he wrote John in January 1895, "the Swedish Lutheran pastors in America are the most papistical of all the world's clergy," and went on to rake them over the coals for their self-satisfaction, hypocrisy, and greed. Behind his lay personal grievances: the pastor in Gowrie had "misused his call" in some unexplained manner "when our noble mother was on her deathbed" and brother Fredrick "did not suit them and so things went for him accordingly."[25] Yet there was more to it than that: Ernest believed in the onward march of Human Progress, led by that emancipated and enlightened elite with which he so proudly identified himself. Mankind must therefore be liberated from the shackles of priestcraft and superstition, above all that habit of mind which saw this world as no more than a transient vale of tears and a preparation for eternity.

Ernest was thus caught up in the epic struggle between religion and science which profoundly divided Western society by the end of the nineteenth century. This cleavage was reflected in the Swedish-American world by the struggle between the churches, with their own societies and periodicals, and the secular clubs, lodges, and publications. The leaders on the one side were the clergy, fighting to protect their flocks from the snares of The World. On the other, the standard-bearers were the editors of the secular Swedish-language newspapers, of whom no more characteristic or influential example could be found than Ernest's friend, Ernst Skarstedt. There is, in fact, a notable similarity in their views—on ultimate human progress, traditional religion, and the more corrupt and lawless aspects of American life—although unlike Ernest, Skarstedt tended to mistrust "meddlesome" social reformers. Both my father and my aunt could remember how "Old Skarstedt" used to come to dinner and bring along his fiddle.[26]

In 1895, while Ernest attacked the Swedish Lutheran clergy in America, he denied that he was either a "separatist" or a "Waldenströmian." He did not, in fact, become irreligious as such and yearned for more satisfying answers to the ultimate mysteries than he could find in the old orthodoxy. He turned to Freemasonry, which was anathema to the traditional churches, and in time advanced to high degree within the Portland lodge. By the mid-1890s he found the message he had been seeking in Theosophy, which combined a belief in an eternal spiritual order with faith in human progress here on earth. He joined the local group and in 1897 he and Jenny traveled down to Point Loma, on San Diego Bay, for the inauguration of the international headquarters of the Theosophical Society.[27] A decade later he would send his son Hildor off to the Theosophists' Raja Yoga Academy at Point Loma, to acquire there the select upbringing which he himself so sorely missed.

In the meantime, he could still appreciate certain aspects of his background, as he did when he and Jenny held a Christmas Eve celebration for the little Swedish colony in North Yamhill, Oregon, in 1894, and "everything was Swedish, except for *lutfisk*, which was not available." Ernest himself sang a hymn, "the same one the late 'Wooden-Shoe Isak' used to sing at *julotta* in August Danielson's schoolhouse."[28] (*Julotta* was the traditional Swedish early-morning Christmas service.)

Some years later, the family dispute over the disposition of the old farm in Lost Grove greatly aroused Ernest, because, he claimed, of the principles at stake. "As far as I am concerned," he wrote John from Portland in April 1902, "I don't care who gets the damned old farm, which was the cause of many tears during the dark days of my captivity there. A regular Bastille of a prison, with only a partial respite when an anemic, woebegone preacher came around to eat chicken and *förmana* [admonish]." He was apprehensive that people in Gowrie disapproved of his having married a singer, who "while she is an artist, . . . is a true, pure woman."[29]

Yet he was still somehow unprepared when he visited Gowrie in 1902–3 in connection with the case—for the first time in a dozen years—to discover how deeply alienated he had now become from his former surroundings. After his return to Oregon he wrote bitterly: "I came back to the home of my childhood, among those I had known since I was a little boy, with all the illusion of that idealistic trust which can only be born in those days of early youth. . . . But from the first I . . . noticed that there was a veil between them and me that finally took the form of suspicion, and I cannot tell you how much that pained me. . . . I feel that a cord has been snapped and never again can I during life think of that place with the same feelings as I did up to that time." He suspected a "superstitious fear" behind this coldness, "for had they not heard I was an unbeliever?" Looking back he saw Gowrie as a "night-mare land," inhabited by "those who sit in the shadow of darkness . . . a living death, a mental palsy, a spiritual sleep—which many fondly hope will end when Gabriel comes to blow his horn."[30] He had evidently done little to endear himself to his old friends and neighbors; it has not yet been forgotten from this last visit of his that when someone asked him, around the potbellied stove in a general store, how he liked Gowrie now, he rolled himself a cigarette and replied, "If you like corn and hogs, it's all right."[31] The local people can hardly have appreciated his particular brand of irony.

The bitterness of his attacks upon Gowrie and the old, rural, and godly Swedish America of his childhood reflect underlying apprehensions of his own personal failings by his fortieth year. Ernest possessed a "brilliant analytical mind," as my aunt has put it, yet was quite devoid of practical common sense when it came to his business and family affairs. When the Panic of 1893 ushered in hard times, he moved his family from Portland out to the small rural community of North Yamhill, where they could raise some fruits and vegetables, keep a cow, and receive other foodstuffs in barter for medical services. Ernest was always generous toward his own and before long a little Swedish colony gathered in North Yamhill, consisting of his sister Frida and brother Emil, Jenny's sister Mina, Emmy—another former member of the Swedish Ladies' Quartette—Andrew Bystrom, who later married Emmy, and his brother Olof, all of whom were out of steady work and more or less lived in the house. In the long run it was simply too much and Jenny took the children back to Portland, realizing that she would have to resume her own career if the family were to be adequately provided for.

By around 1898 the family was back in the Portland house. In the meantime Jenny found singing engagements; among other things she sang, suitably decked out, "Columbia, Gem of the Ocean" at ceremonies for the local volunteers departing for the Spanish-American war. In time she found a patron among Portland's leading socialites who provided funds for her to prepare for an operatic career during the next couple of years in Paris and Italy. By 1902 she was singing leading roles in the opera houses of Stockholm, Christiania, Berlin, London, New York, and elsewhere, under the stage name, Jenny Norelli. In 1914 her great opportunity came when she was engaged as the prima donna of the Dresden Opera, but the First World War intervened. At that very time, too, her hearing began to fail. Thus "La Norelli's" promising career ended at its very height. She eventually turned to teaching and from 1920 had a highly respected voice studio in Seattle.[32]

All of this meant that Jenny could seldom be with Ernest or with the children, who in her absence were largely raised by her sister Mina and by Emmy and Andrew Bystrom. Yet the love between them never wavered and they never ceased to look forward to the day when they would no longer have to be separated. In the meantime, Jenny not only provided for her children but also very largely for her husband as well.

Ernest did not in the least begrudge Jenny either her career or her long absences. He was, on the contrary, sincerely happy over her successes and saw in her a splendid example of the "warlike Svea tribe," as he proudly described her to a niece in 1922. He meanwhile sat at his rolltop desk in his cluttered office in Portland, waiting for an occasional patient, convinced that the local clergy had done their best to ruin his practice. In actuality, he was now far less concerned with medicine—which seemed to him to boil down to listening to old women complain about imaginary ills—than with a variety of exciting projects that sprang from his fertile and restless mind. He could spend entire days over the details of Masonic symbolism or in talking Democratic politics. He invented his own system of Swedish shorthand. In an undated letter to John he revealed that he and three partners were seeking to raise "a couple of thousand" to go down to Mexico or Central America, find "10 thousand acres cheap," and make their killing in cacao, tobacco, vanilla, rubber, and coffee. Nothing further is heard of this scheme, but in December 1903 he was trying to raise $165.60, at any interest, from John and Victor, to take advantage of the great opportunity of his life to acquire an interest in several promising cinnabar claims staked out in the Oregon mountains by a Portland mining consultant named Otto M. Rosendale —probably a Swede whose original name would have been Rosendal.[33]

Nothing apparently came of this project either but from at least this point on Ernest's consuming interest was mining and metallurgy. He now spent varying lengths of time in mining towns in northern Washington and even visited Sitka, Alaska, around 1910 on some mining business. By 1914 he was increasingly occupied with the invention of mining machinery, hoping to strike it rich. There is mention of "ore-saving machines" in 1924. But the great project of his later years was his "Forno" electric copper smelter. Various mining companies were interested and for some years he lived largely on the advance promotion money they paid him. Despite delays and obstacles, he was increasingly optimistic that he was on the verge of his great breakthrough. With his daughter Margit he would expatiate upon the genteel and luxurious life they would live when the big money started coming in.[34]

As he reached his sixties Ernest seems to have begun to mellow somewhat toward the background he had rebelled so fiercely against in his restless middle years. Thus he could reminisce fondly in 1922 about the Midsummer celebrations at Bullebo or

the following year recall with amusement how the chief of the
Tama Indians used to come to the farm in Lost Grove to eat
when he was in the neighborhood and would then let Ernest
ride his pony—until it once got away from him and ran all the
way home to the Tama encampment, fifteen miles away. He
was fond of telling humorous stories, which now became more
good-natured than ironic.[35]

In the meantime, however, his health began to fail. Already
sometime before 1918 he developed Buerger's disease, a con-
striction of circulation to the legs, aggravated by the use of
tobacco, which Ernest could never manage to give up. The pain
from a toe he had once frozen in a mining camp eventually became so unbearable that he cut it off himself one night with his
penknife. In the fall of 1924 his left leg became gangrenous and
had to be amputated. He was soon up again and was occupied
with negotiations for starting a company to put his electric
smelter into operation when he died, suddenly and peacefully,
alone in his room in Portland on 3 February 1926, at the age of
sixty-seven.[36]

Although he had not been a success in business or as a pro-
vider for his family, Jenny had written their son over a year
earlier, "his intentions were always right." To John she now
wrote, "Ernest and I remained true lovers all our life together."
Devotedly she tried to carry on his work, to get the copper
smelter built and into operation, but it turned out that Ernest's
voluminous notes and diagrams using his own personal shorthand were virtually undecipherable, even to the experts.[37] His
secret was lost with his death.

In writing to John in Gowrie to tell him of Ernest's passing,
Jenny was especially concerned about how Sophie might take
the news, in view of her many recent bereavements. Following
Victor's retirement as postmaster in Gowrie, Sophie and he
moved to Fort Dodge to be near their children and built a home
there in 1915. Only three years later Victor died, in February
1918. Of their eleven children it will be remembered that six had
died in infancy in Lost Grove; two of the others followed not
long after their father, George in 1921 and Frank in 1923. Emil

had gone in 1917, Frida in 1925, and now Ernest, whom she had always been fond of, in 1926. She was no longer well herself. She suffered badly from rheumatism and in 1926 had a stroke. Yet Sophie remained cheerful and serene, never losing her old sense of humor, to the end. She died in Fort Dodge in 1927, aged eighty-one. She is described as tall, spare, and clear-eyed: the very type of the pioneer woman.[38]

In 1910 John retired from active farming and left his place to his son, Theodore. John and Carrie moved into Gowrie, where they built themselves a house catercornered across the street from the Lutheran church. On a large lot in back John put up a greenhouse and cultivated a sizable garden and berry patch. He was now, according to his letterhead, "John T. Svenson, Horticulturist," and he was able to carry on a tidy little business with his produce. Theodore, his wife Selma, and their children, Clifford and Margerie, were close by on the farm, yet John may well have been thinking of his own aged father's last years when he later maintained that he would not want to live with his son's family.[39]

In 1928, when John was eighty, he returned to Sweden for a visit. We can imagine the contrast in his eyes between the Swedish America Line's majestic and commodious new *Gripsholm*, on which he now sailed, and the primitive early steam vessel with which he had last crossed the Atlantic on his way to America in 1867. But this would be only a foretaste of the great contrast he would experience between the Sweden he was now visiting as a tourist and the land he had left as an emigrant over a half century before. John quickly made his way to the place of his birth. Fru Eddy Gustafsson of Vimmerby is the daughter of the family which then leased Bullebo farm. She recalls:

> He came to Bullebo one evening in the summer of 1928 and asked if he could stay for a few days, for he had been born at Bullebo and would so much like to visit his old childhood home. The answer, naturally, was yes, and he stayed with us for two weeks. He became like a dear relative to us during these days. Tears came to our eyes more than once when he spoke about everything he recognized after sixty years' ab-

sence. He remembered which fruit trees his father had planted, he could remember rocks, the buildings were the same, there was even the same wallpaper in a room on the second floor. When a few days had passed I remember he said, "Now I see that I will have to change my ideas about Sweden. I thought it was the same as when I left, that the old men went around in their patched, homespun trousers, but a lot has changed in sixty years." One day he went off cheerfully to Karsnäs to visit his relatives but came back very sad, for they had not wanted anything to do with him. He said, "We became poor before we left for America and that must have been why."[40]

After leaving Bullebo, John continued to correspond with the leaseholder, Emil Carlsson, and his family. His letters show how he found old Ida Lindbäck, "the only person I can remember who is still living," in the bookstore in Vimmerby, visited in Vederslöv, near Växjö, a returned Swedish American who had once lived in Gowrie, continued to Mjölby, Linköping, and Stockholm, and ended his stay with a boat trip on the Göta Canal back to Gothenburg, from whence he took the *Gripsholm* home. Before returning to Gowrie, he looked up in Chicago a certain Dahlquist who had emigrated from Djursdala the year before he had. From Bullebo, Emil Carlsson wrote at the end of the year, "You left happy memories among all you came in contact with in our old land."[41]

With John's return to his birthplace the circle of his family's odyssey was somehow now completed and he could go back to his home on the prairie to live out his last few years in the community he had helped to build. As for his cold reception at Karsnäs he later recalled that he had arrived there while a revival meeting was being held within—John thought it sounded more like an auction—that his cousin Matilda was eighty-four years old and nearly blind, and that the folk at Karsnäs had probably misunderstood who he was and why he had come. In his letters to Bullebo, John meanwhile wrote of his children and grandchildren, of his garden, of prices, wages, and the onset of the Great Depression. He spoke of birthdays, anniversaries, the tearing down of the old wooden church he had helped to build in 1880–81, in Brother Fredrick's day, and the construction of a new brick edifice, where, John noted, he seldom went any more.[42]

John's letters to Bullebo during his last years show how keen his memory still remained. He proved an indispensable source of information to the editor of the *Gowrie News*, Armanis F. Patton, and to the Swedish-American journalist and author, O. M. Nelson, when both were gathering material on the history of the Lost Grove and Gowrie communities in the 1920s and 1930s.[43] He meanwhile continued to work in his garden until a few days before he died in May 1933, at the age of 84.[44] Caroline followed two years later.

The last to go was Oscar, who remained on the old farm: a calm, easygoing man of quiet faith and courage. He died, aged seventy-nine years, in August 1935, in the same house where the old patriarch, Sven Svenson, had left this earthly scene a quarter century earlier.[45] His wife, Maria, lived on until 1941. Oscar and she lie in the hilltop graveyard in Lost Grove, surrounded by their own, by those who had lived through and experienced the great Atlantic sea change.

11

Epilogue

The descendants of Sven and Sara Maria Svenson are now numerous and widely scattered. Several of them still live in or around Gowrie, or elsewhere in Iowa. Others are to be found in Illinois, Missouri, Nebraska, Texas, Arizona, California, Alaska, and probably other states as well. Counting those now retired, they presently include—to my knowledge—a farmer, a service station operator, an electrician, a machinist, a nurse, a beauty parlor operator, a postal clerk, a librarian, a fashion artist, a technical writer, a university professor, several business people, schoolteachers, and housewives, and children of all ages. Some are quite prosperous, some in modest circumstances. They are in many walks of life and represent at least a partial cross section of American society.

The historian Franklin D. Scott rightly reminds us that those who came to America were not *born* to leave their old surroundings and live new lives in a new land.[1] For some, circumstances conspired to encourage such a break with the past. Faced with this challenge, some—like Sven Svenson and his family—were prepared to leave. Others were not.

In mulling over the consequences of their fateful choice we cannot help asking whether it was the right one. Surely they could have found ways to remain in the land of their birth, if they had been determined to do so, and one member did eventually return to it. When we seek to compare the quality of life of their descendents in America today with that of their Swedish relatives, we may wonder which have been the more fortunate in the long run. Yet one thing is certain: neither Swedes nor

Swedish Americans would have been able to do as well for themselves as they have if the great migration had not taken place, opening up new opportunities for those who left and relieving the pressures of overpopulation and poverty for those who stayed.

Sven and his family encountered both good and bad fortune in their new homeland. They did not come to America expecting to "whittle gold with a carving knife," as the old emigrant song put it. They sought a decent livelihood through honest labor, and this they found. Still, contrary to the old patriotic stereotype, the immigrant's way in American life was often a hard one and there is a strong element of tragedy in the story of the Svenson family.

There was Sven himself, who wanted nothing better in life than to be a respected and well-to-do farmer in his ancestral Småland, like his father and brothers, but felt compelled to sell everything and start all over again in a new land at the age of fifty, rather than face the prospect of impoverishment for himself and his family. There was Sara Maria, who never ceased to grieve for her old home at Bullebo. Fredrick, who bore his heavy cross of ill health and poverty for the greater glory of God. Ludvig, who died in poverty in Colorado. Sophie, who lost six of her eleven children in infancy and two more in adulthood before she died. Louisa, whose young life ended so early, leaving scarcely a trace behind her. Ernest, whose ambitious dreams and promising talents met with so much frustration. Irving, Frida, and Emil, who never really found their places in society.

Yet they did not blame America for their ills. They knew that their failures derived above all from their own weaknesses, just as their successes were won through their own abilities. For these too were a part of the picture. Sven could listen to the corn growing on warm summer evenings. Sara Maria and he could see some of their children acquire education and social standing they could hardly have hoped for in Sweden. Fredrick's labors in the Lord's vineyard gave him strength. Sophie, despite all her trials, never lost her calm courage, good nature, and zest for life. Tilda eventually had the chance to make something of herself in the nation's capital. Frida lived a colorful and adventurous life and possessed her own robust wit. Ernest, for all his bitterness at times, had a rare—if sometimes cutting— sense of humor and was genuinely gratified by the successes of his wife and children. John lived a long and rewarding life, enriched by his happy marriage, many interests, and wide reading. Oscar remained close to the soil he had tilled since his early youth. Their lives contained dramatic contrasts of fortune. Yet together they exemplify much in the life of the young American republic in their time, with its enormous vitality, its breathtaking development, its exciting opportunities, its gaping pitfalls.

Having made their home in America, they became American. But what does this mean in practice? American historians have in the past traditionally tended to look at our society as a "melting pot," in which each immigrant nationality has automatically lost its distinguishing cultural traits as rapidly as it was capable of doing so. According to this view, the Swedes and other Scandinavians, being northern European, Germanic, and Protestant, were considered particularly desirable immigrants, since they were generally believed to assimilate more quickly, easily, and willingly than virtually any other group in America. More recently, during the 1960s and 1970s, this interpretation has been challenged by an "Ethnic Renaissance," whose proponents have shown that assimilation to the prevailing Anglo-Saxon pattern proceeded neither rapidly nor easily within any immigrant group and that significant residues of their original heritages have remained, even after they have lost the more obvious traits of ethnicity.[2] Much of this dispute has created more heat than light, in my opinion. The fact of basic assimilation is undeniable, even if each group has contributed something to the evolving pattern of American culture. The significant questions must therefore be: how fast, how selective, how complete?

What does the example of the Svenson family tell us in this regard? Each of its members acclimated to the new society, yet in a variety of ways. Some adapted themselves as little as was necessary in their own circumstances; others sought to blend as completely as possible into the mainstream of American life. Some of them scarcely felt assimilation to be a problem; for others it posed painful dilemmas, never completely resolved.

Marriage and intermarriage are rightly considered a major indicator of the rate and degree of assimilation. Of Sven and Sara Maria's eleven children, five remained single. Of the six who married (including Fredrick, who was married three times), all took spouses who were either Swedish-born, like themselves, or born in America of Swedish parents. Of their children—the second generation after Sven and Sara Maria—nine were married but only three of them to persons of Swedish background, so far as I can determine, while the rest had spouses of old American, German, or Irish derivation. The over forty known marriages of the third and fourth generations include only three or four spouses of evidently Swedish origin, while the remainder have had surnames at least that have been Anglo-Saxon, German, Polish, Norwegian, or Danish.

We have seen that while most of the Svenson children anglicized their Christian names, some of them retained their original family name, while others took another Swedish name (Westerdal), or adopted anglicized or Anglo-Saxon names (Swainson, Westerdale, West, Barton). This matter of names is a revealing sign of their varying desire and ability to assimilate. All meanwhile continued to use their native language to a greater or lesser extent throughout their lives, all of the second generation was brought up with it, and some of the third generation is still able to use it with varying degrees of fluency. Similarly, most of Sven and Sara Maria's children remained professing Lutherans, while those of their descendants who are church members belong partly to the Lutheran, partly to other Protestant denominations.[3] It should be added that there are those of the third and fourth generations who have English names, are not Lutheran, and speak no Swedish, but still serve *lutfisk* on Christmas Eve and have even persuaded their non-Swedish relatives to like it.

These are, however, the outward attributes of ethnicity. In

the early years of this century when the generational stresses caused by assimilation were at their height within Swedish America, dire warnings were heard from the pulpit and the Swedish-language press that if the old language and creed should be lost, nothing would remain of the Swedish heritage in America. From the vantage point of the third generation, I am convinced that this has not been so, that there are attitudes and values—ways of looking at things and of reacting to them— that still live on among Americans of Swedish background. If it can be explained in no other way, I find that we feel at home with each other.

There is an old Arab proverb which says, "Men resemble their time more than they do their fathers."[4] Yet the more I have studied this family, the more I wonder about this. When my father first met Clifford Swenson in 1957, both were middle-aged and from different parts of the country. Even so, both of them, and my mother as well, were astonished at how similar they were in appearance, manner, and attitude. I have repeatedly had similar experiences in discovering relatives, near and distant, in the United States and in Sweden. From at least the mid-eighteenth century on, a family profile seems to emerge. It includes, I believe, a stubborn individuality in the face of what others may think; a certain restlessness, curiosity, and adaptability; a relative indifference to physical discomfort and hardship; a sense of family, combined with a degree of intransigence and irascibility that could frequently lead to conflict with others, sadly enough often between members of the family itself. For better or for worse, both its strengths and weaknesses have run to form.

Edmund Burke said in the eighteenth century that life in society was an ongoing partnership between the living, the dead, and those yet to be born.[5] To study the Svenson family in Sweden and America, from as far back as the preserved records will allow down to the present day, reveals a continuity no less impressive than that of the national group to which it belonged and of which it was so representative. This study has helped me to understand who and what I am, and why. It has shown how a family continues to live its own life and follow its own lines of development, from generation to generation, despite all changes of landscape, custom, language, dogma, occupation, ethnic admixture, and name. Circumstances change beyond recognition. Individuals die. Some do not marry or have children of their own. The family endures and its history continues.

Problems and Sources
Notes
Index

Problems and Sources

It has been my intention not only to tell what I have found but to show how I managed to find it. I have thus sought to write history "with the works showing." I hope others may also feel inspired to pursue their own family histories and may be able to benefit from the example I have provided. With this in mind, some further comment on problems and sources may be helpful.

It should be clear by now that sheer luck plays an enormous role. I have had remarkably good luck, in locating both written documents and persons whose living memory and expertise I have been able to draw upon. By way of example I need only mention Lennart Setterdahl's discovery of Jonas Öhrn's grave in New Sweden's Methodist burial ground or the finding of the lost letters from John Svenson to Emil Carlsson at Bullebo from 1928 to 1932, in a desk drawer in Vimmerby. You can also have bad luck, as did a Danish friend of mine; he learned to his delight of a batch of old family letters, but when he asked for them he was told that they had been burned up only two weeks before. The mind boggles at the thought!

But good luck is often the reward for dogged persistence. My files at this point are stuffed with correspondence, consisting largely of vain and fruitless inquiries. But it is all worthwhile when repeated efforts finally turn up the desired bits of information. I wrote, for instance, to the National Archives in Washington, D.C., and to the state archives of Illinois and Iowa trying to locate the Civil War service record for Ludvig Daniel *Svenson* (or *Svensson*, or *Swainson*). All to no avail. It was only a couple of years later when I tried *Swanson* that I finally got what I was looking for. (As we have seen, the problem of names can be particularly tricky!)

Dogged persistence can, however, sometimes lead you on a wild goose chase. In scanning the muster roll of Company C, Forty-third Illinois Volunteer Infantry Regiment, the unit in which Ludvig served, I was astonished to find the name of none other than Victor Nelson. A preliminary inquiry to the Illinois State Archives in Springfield showed that he was a native of Sweden, had been residing in Andover, Illinois, at the time of his enlistment, and served from September 1861 to September 1864. Everything fell into place beautifully. Sven Svenson's son-in-law was known to have first immigrated to America before the Civil War, was the right age in 1861, and had been living in northwestern Illinois at the time. He had surely known the Svensons since his childhood in Odensvi, could have persuaded Ludvig to join his old company when the latter came over in 1864, settled together with known veterans of the same unit in Lost Grove Township, and so on. The only trouble was that Pvt. Victor Nelson of Company C turned out to be someone else altogether. His service record at the National Archives in Washington showed that he later became a farmer in Orion, Illinois, was committed to an insane asylum in 1887, and died in 1906. An elaborate and cunning theoretical construct went down in flames.

Your results will naturally reflect chance factors. In my case I happened to find a whole cache of family letters from the year 1876. Fortunately that year proved to be a significant one in the family's history. Similarly, I was able to locate a good deal of material on five persons in particular: Peter Anderson, Jonas Öhrn, Sven Svenson, Sven Fredrik Westerdal, and Ernest (Svenson) Barton. Here too I consider myself fortunate, for together they make a fortuitous combination, well worth highlighting in my account, even though I would have liked to know more about some of the others.

For research into an immigrant family a command of the old language is almost indispensable. There are definite limits to what you can accomplish without it, even with a good helper who can use it. A project of this kind is ample reason in itself to learn the language, and the more thoroughly the better. Not only was most of the Svenson family correspondence in Swedish, for instance, but I would surely have misunderstood some of the earlier letters in faulty English had I not been able to visualize the Swedish words and constructions that the writers obviously had in mind.

The starting point for a family history must be the gathering of oral information from older persons with long memories. I have discussed this aspect, among others, in a brief article on local historical research, "What Can I Do?" in the *Swedish Pioneer Historical Quarterly*, 26 (1975), 211–14. This is a task that can never begin too soon, for the old-timers can leave us at any time, taking with them information that can never be replaced. It is important in interviewing them to think out and note down ahead the questions you want to ask them. At the same time you should let them reminisce freely, which may bring up points that had not occurred to you. A tape recorder can be useful, since it can preserve exact turns of phrase and tones of voice, the significance of which may not be immediately apparent.

Speaking of taped interviews, the most remarkable one I obtained was from a hundred-year-old relative, Ernst Pettersson, in Ankarsrum, Småland, whom I learned about in 1975. As I could not visit him myself at the time, his grandson interviewed him on my behalf. He died the following year at the age of one hundred one. Although he was unable to contribute much information of direct relevance to this study, his mind was spry and his memory excellent. The tape cassette with his recollections and a letter he wrote to me are among the most treasured documents in my collection.

The problem with oral information, especially when it consists of stories or traditions heard long ago from others, is that it is often mixed up and misleading. It has led me off onto the wrong trail more than once. Yet even scrambled information of this kind can have its value, for it usually contains its grain of truth, however well it may be disguised. Jonas Öhrn in particular was surrounded by a thick layer of legend. How did Dad ever get the idea that he had been a "captain"? It eventually occurred to me that Dad's *mother's* uncle, Carl Ludvig Norelius from Söderhamn in Hälsingland, who lived from 1817 to 1863, had indeed been a sea captain and may have been in America "in Andrew Jackson's time," possibly even visiting Fort Dearborn. If Jonas Öhrn had not been in America quite that early, he did come over already in "Millard Fillmore's time," which was early

enough in the history of the Swedish emigration. And, unbe-
known to Dad, Peter Anderson and his family had come over
already six years before Öhrn.

Yet there remains another—admittedly slight—possibility regarding the origin of this particular story. It eventually came to
my attention that a Swedish seaman, allegedly born in Gothenburg around 1780, enlisted in November 1814 in the U.S. Army
under the name of Andrew L. (or Andrew S.) Fagerstrom, when
Andrew Jackson commanded American troops in the War of
1812 against Great Britain. (See Nils William Olsson, "Swedish
Enlistments in the U.S. Army before 1850," *Swedish Pioneer
Historical Quarterly*, 1 [1951], 11.) It is not impossible that he
might then or at some other time have been at Fort Dearborn.
While the name Fagerström is not altogether uncommon in
Sweden, it was a well-established one in Odensvi parish and is
to be found among the forebears of Christina Anderson and her
brother, Anders Edvard Fagerström, Victor Nelson, and Lena
Cajsa Öhrn (nee Hornwall). Although this "Andrew Fagerstrom" (Anders Fagerström) may have arrived in America from
the seaport of Gothenburg, it is not unlikely that he was actually
born elsewhere, or that he could in any case have been related
to the Odensvi Fagerströms. The idea that this part of the Öhrn
legend may have derived ultimately from him is thus an intrigu-
ing one.

Sven Svenson's wife did not die "in the shade of a covered
wagon," as Dad seemed to recall, but Öhrn's third wife, Johanna, very likely did. If Öhrn did not go back to Sweden to
visit, thereby encouraging Sven and his family to emigrate,
Victor Nelson did. It is hardly surprising that as a young child
Dad should have mixed up what he heard about different forebears he had never seen.

Clifford Swenson's story that Öhrn had *owned* 160 acres in
what was later to be the heart of Chicago could easily have had
its origin in some sharper's attempt to *sell* him such a property
when he was passing through the city on his way out to New
Sweden, Iowa. But what of the Indian half-breed woman Clifford had heard his father, Theodore, mention? It is not impossible that such a person figured in some episode in Öhrn's life,
although it seems more likely that mistaken identity is involved
here. I have since discovered striking similarities between parts

of the Öhrn legend and the life of Jacob Fahlström, a fur trapper celebrated as Minnesota's earliest Swedish settler, in particular Fahlström's Indian wife and his sizable property in what was later the middle of *St. Paul*. (See Theodore A. Norelius, "The First Swede in Minnesota," *Swedish Pioneer Historical Quarterly*, 8 [1957], 107–14.) This is a story which Theodore Swenson could very well have heard. The point is that each of the Öhrn stories surely contains its grain of truth—if only it could be tracked down.

Any family letters, diaries, accounts, photographs, or other such materials that can be found are naturally of the greatest value. Even the most apparently insignificant things, such as an old Swedish book with the name, "Irving F. Westerdale," inscribed in it, or Ernest's prescription pad from Omaha, or a menu from John's return trip from Sweden on the S.S. *Gripsholm* in 1928, were all able to give me useful clues. This leads in turn to a point worth making: the importance of going back over your material repeatedly, since as you acquire more background you will discover new things in it you had overlooked before.

In addition to family papers, there are public records of many kinds. The use of such documentation for Swedish-American genealogy is discussed in Nils William Olsson's brief but helpful guide, "Tracing Your Swedish Ancestry," in the *Swedish Pioneer Historical Quarterly*, 13 (1962), 160–74, which has also been reprinted in revised form as a pamphlet under the same title by the Royal Swedish Ministry of Foreign Affairs in 1965 and 1974. A fuller treatment of the Swedish sources is provided by Carl-Erik Johansson in *Cradled in Sweden: A Practical Help to Genealogical Research in Swedish Records* (Logan, Utah: Everton Publishers, 1972) and Ulf Beijbom, *Släkt- och hembygdsforskning* (Stockholm: Natur och Kultur, 1977). The Genealogical Association in Salt Lake City, which is affiliated with the Mormon church, possesses a complete microfilm of all Swedish church records and individual reels can be borrowed through the cooperation of the local Mormon congregations.

Vital statistics in Sweden have been kept longer and are surely more complete and better organized than anywhere else in the world. It has been the responsibility of parish pastors, since at least the earlier eighteenth century, to record all births, baptisms, confirmations, marriages, deaths, burials, and moves into or out of the parish, giving places of prior or later residence. Records of taxes, property transfers, litigation, inheritances, military service, literacy, education, and similar matters complete the picture. Inquiries concerning church records less than one hundred years old should be made to the pastor of the parish in question; those involving other documents should be addressed to the provincial archive (*landsarkiv*) for the region. (These archives and the areas they cover are listed with addresses in the Olsson guide, referred to above.)

The essential keys to using these Swedish materials for genealogical research are the *year* of emigration and the *parish* in which the emigrant was officially residing at the time of departure. When these details are known, it is possible to discover the main events of the individual's life, from the time of emigration back to his birth, and to trace his ancestry, usually through several generations. If you do nothing else at this point, obtain these pieces of information if there is anyone still living who can provide them. If they have been lost, it may take much searching and considerable ingenuity to recover them; this often proves the most difficult problem a researcher has to solve.

American public records are, unfortunately, much scantier, more widely dispersed, and difficult to locate. Systems of recordkeeping often vary from state to state. We have no sure way, as in Sweden, to trace a person's changing places of domicile. The most basic place to begin your search is nonetheless the county courthouse, which generally contains records of births, marriages, deaths, property transfers, litigation, and the probating of wills. I have been able to make good use of such material particularly in my treatment of Jonas Öhrn in Jefferson County, Iowa. State archives contain the county census takers' reports, giving the names, ages, occupations, places of birth, and evaluated property of all county residents. In using such material, it is best to search through the actual documents yourself, rather than have someone else do it for you, since foreign names were often distorted almost beyond recognition by early census takers. Reports for the ten-year national census were sent to Washington, D.C., and are deposited in the National Archives. National census material is accessible for research after seventy years, thus at present through the census of 1890.

Service records for men in state volunteer regiments up to and including the Civil War are kept by both state and national archives. For other wars they are located in the National Archives. Records kept by churches, chambers of commerce, private associations, businesses, or cemeteries can yield additional details, as can the back files of local or Swedish-American newspapers, not least their obituary columns. A helpful guide to the use of the American materials is E. Kay Kirkham, *Research in American Genealogy* (Salt Lake City: Deseret Book Company, 1956). For research methods, Allan Lichtman's *Your Family History* (New York: Vintage Books, 1978) may be recommended.

The history of a family becomes more interesting, both for the researcher and for others, if it goes beyond the bare genealogical outline and relates to the times and places involved. Where specific, documented details may be lacking for the persons you are studying, your knowledge of the historical background can help you to recreate a plausible picture of their activities and concerns. My own years of reading on both Swedish and American history have been no less important to this account than my detailed family research.

The sources for such background are unlimited, but let me end by suggesting a few of the most important works dealing specifically with Swedish emigration and Swedes in North America. Three older classics remain indispensable: for the factors behind emigration, Florence E. Janson, *The Background of Swedish Immigration, 1840–1930* (University of Chicago Press, 1931); on settlement patterns and the geographic distribution of Swedes in the United States and Canada, Helge Nelson, *The Swedes and the Swedish Settlements in North America*, 2 vols (Lund: Gleerup, 1943), the second volume of which contains valuable maps; and on religious and related cultural life, George M. Stephenson, *The Religious Aspects of Swedish Immigration* (Minneapolis: University of Minnesota Press, 1932). All three contain extensive bibliographies.

The fullest source of bibliographical information is meanwhile O. Fritiof Ander, *The Cultural Heritage of the Swedish Immigrant: Selected References* (Rock Island, Ill.: Augustana Book Concern, 1956), which may be supplemented down to the present with the book reviews and notices in the *Swedish Pioneer Historical Quarterly*, since 1950, itself a mine of information. Note also the supplement to Vol. 22 (1971), *Index to Volumes I through XX, 1950–1969*, an invaluable aid when searching for specific details. Harald Runblom and Hans Norman have edited a compendium of recent, important research in Sweden, *From Sweden to America: A History of the Migration*, Studia Historica Upsaliensia, 74 (Uppsala: Almqvist och Wiksell; Minneapolis: University of Minnesota Press, 1976). My own *Letters from the Promised Land: Swedes in America, 1840–1914* (Minneapolis: University of Minnesota Press, 1975) is an anthology of representative immigrant letters in English translation, with commentaries that provide a brief summary of the migration.

For the Swedish background, Stewart Oakley, *A Short History of Sweden* (New York: Praeger, 1966) provides a good, brief, narrative introduction, while Ingvar Andersson, *A History of Sweden*, trans. Carolyn Hannay (London: Weidenfeld & Nicolson, 1955), and Franklin D. Scott, *Sweden: The Nation's History* (Minneapolis: University of Minnesota Press, 1977) are more analytical and detailed.

Reference works are essential. I have made constant use of the encyclopedia, *Svensk uppslagsbok*, 32 vols. (Malmö: Förlagshuset Norden AB, 1948–55), which in addition to clarifying innumerable points contains excellent maps of Swedish provinces and towns. I cannot overstress the importance of good maps, even though they can never serve as a substitute for actually visiting the locations involved and soaking up their particular atmosphere. There are several good cartographic series, such as the *Topografisk karta över Sverige*, the U.S. Geological Survey, and the county maps put out by various state departments of transportation. The *Ekonomisk karta över Sverige* and the local plat books maintained in the county courthouses in the United States are useful for determining property ownership at different periods. Biographical dictionaries can also often be a valuable resource, including those covering special categories of persons, such as the clergy of individual Swedish dioceses, prominent Swedish Americans in particular states, or the established residents in American counties or townships.

Notes

1. The Search

1. There is often some confusion in the spelling of Swedish immigrants' names. I have generally followed the customary practice of the immigrants themselves of dropping the second *s* in names ending with *-son* after coming to America. Thus *Svensson* before 1867 becomes *Svenson* after that year. Similarly the Swedish letters *å*, *ä*, and *ö* usually turned into *a* or *o*. Theodore Svenson died in 1962, Selma in 1966.
2. Summarisk redogörelse för folkmängden i Djursdala annex, församling af Tunaläns o. Sevedes prosteri, Calmar län under år 1867; also for 1866.
3. My *Letters from the Promised Land: Swedes in America, 1840–1914* (Minneapolis: University of Minnesota Press, 1975).
4. [O. M. Nelson], *Swedish Settlements in Iowa and Western Illinois* (n.p.: privately published by the author, 1939).
5. Ibid., p. 51.
6. L. Bygdén, *Härnösands stifts herdaminnen*, 4 vols. (Uppsala: Almqvist och Wiksell, 1923–26), I, 67–68.

2. All the Way Back to Noah

1. Vilhelm Moberg, *Utvandrarna* (Stockholm: Bonnier, 1951), Ch. 1; English translation by Gustaf Lannestock, *The Emigrants* (New York: Simon and Schuster, 1951). See also Lars-Olof Larsson, *Historia om Småland* (Växjö: Diploma, 1974).
2. Marcus Lee Hansen, *The Atlantic Migration, 1607–1860* (New York: Torchbooks-Harper, 1961), xiv–xv.
3. D. A. Peterson, "From Östergötland to Iowa," *Swedish Pioneer Historical Quarterly*, 22 (1971), 142; also in my *Letters from the Promised Land*, p. 56.
4. Ernest O. Barton to a niece, 19 December 1922. I have excerpts copied from the original letter by my father. Although the niece is not identified on this copy, it was Ellen Nelson Watkins, the daughter

of Sophie Svenson, whom my father visited in Fort Dodge, Iowa, in 1960.
5. Ibid.
6. Ibid.
7. *Fil. dr.* Torsten Andersson, Uppsala, to Karin Augustinson, 23 October 1967. On Loxbo (formerly often spelled Låxbo or Låxby), see Johan Fredrik Cornelius, *Beskrifning öfver Södra Vi Socken* (Vimmerby, 1885), reprinted in *Södra Vi-krönikan*, 4 (1968), 8.
8. Letter to me from Karin Augustinson, Ödeshög, 10 March 1976.
9. Letter to me from Karin Augustinson, Ödeshög, August 1976.
10. Gerd and Bengt Einerstam, "Bland fornminnen och sägner i Södra Vi," *Södra Vi-krönikan*, 3 (1967), 39.
11. Letters to me from Karin Augustinson, Ödeshög, 10 March, 14 May, August, 10 September 1976; genealogical chart prepared by Elsa Östblom, Vadstena, 20 September 1977.
12. Letter to me from Karin Augustinson, Ödeshög, August 1976.
13. Letter to me from Karin Augustinson, Ödeshög, 4 November 1975.
14. Cf. the traditions and superstitions described in Helge Åkerhielm, "Swedish Christmas," in Ewert Cagner et al., *Swedish Christmas* (Gothenburg: Tre Tryckare, 1955), pp. 21–90. Ethnology, the study of folk culture, is highly developed in Sweden, as witnessed by the Nordic Museum and its separate "Folk Memory Collection" (*Folkminnessamlingen*), and the Skansen open-air museum in Stockholm, as well as innumerable local history societies and museums throughout the country. We have little to compare with them in the United States. My friend, Sigvard Cederroth in Uppsala, has over the years collected thousands of peasant sayings and proverbs in the province of Uppland alone.
15. Letter to me from Karin Augustinson, Ödeshög, 14 May 1976.
16. On the Swedish peasantry during the sixteenth and seventeenth centuries, see Eli F. Heckscher, *An Economic History of Sweden* (Cambridge, Mass.: Harvard University Press, 1954); and Enoch Ingers and Sten Carlsson, *Bonden i svensk historia*, 3 vols. (Stockholm: LTs Förlag, 1949–56), I.
17. Letters to me from Karin Augustinson, Ödeshög, 10 March 1974 (quoted), 14 February 1976. I am indebted to Miss Augustinson for photocopies of the estate inventories of Stephan Olufsson and others discussed in this and the following chapter, the originals of which are preserved in the Vadstena *landsarkiv*.
18. Ernest Barton to niece, 19 December 1922; letter to me from Karin Augustinson, Ödeshög, 28 September 1973.
19. Letter to me from Gösta Karlsson, Djursdala, 22 October 1972.
20. See my article, "Late Gustavian Autocracy in Sweden: Gustav IV Adolf and His Opponents, 1792–1809," *Scandinavian Studies*, 46 (1974), 272–74.
21. See my article, "Popular Education in Eighteenth-Century Sweden: Theory and Practice," in James A. Leith, ed., *Aspects of Education*

in the Eighteenth Century, Studies in Voltaire and the Eighteenth Century, 167 (Oxford, 1977), 523–41.
22. Letter to me from Kerstin Olsson, Södra Vi, 26 September 1973.
23. On Gustaf Unonius and the Pine Lake colony, see George M. Stephenson, trans. and ed., *Letters Relating to Gustaf Unonius and the Early Swedish Settlers in Wisconsin*, Augustana Historical Society Publications, 7 (Rock Island, Ill., 1937); Gustaf Unonius, *A Pioneer in Northwest America, 1841–1858*, trans. J. Oscar Backlund, ed. Nils William Olsson, 2 vols. (Minneapolis: University of Minnesota Press, 1950, 1960), I. On Swedish emigration prior to 1841, see Nils William Olsson, *Swedish Passenger Arrivals in New York, 1820–1850* (Chicago: Swedish Pioneer Historical Society, 1967); and Axel Friman, "Swedish Emigration to North America, 1820–1850," *Swedish Pioneer Historical Quarterly*, 27 (1976), 153–77.

3. First Link with the New World

1. This account of Peter Andersson's life in Sweden is based, unless otherwise noted, upon information from church records preserved at Vadstena *landsarkiv*, gathered by Karin Augustinson and passed on to me in conversations between May and August 1977.
2. On Ogestad manor, see Ada Rydström, *Boken om Tjust*, 4 vols. (Västervik: C. O. Ekblad och Co., 1912–25), IV, 114–15.
3. Olsson, *Swedish Passenger Arrivals in New York*, pp. 64–65. Quite by chance, the sample of a passport journal, reproduced in Nils William Olsson, *Tracing Your Swedish Ancestry*, rev. ed. (Stockholm: Royal Ministry of Foreign Affairs, 1974), p. 15, is that for Kalmar between 28 February and 27 June 1845, which includes the entry for the Anderson family.
4. *Najaden* (Karlskrona), 12 June 1845; *Aftonbladet* (Stockholm), 27 June 1845. Cf. George M. Stephenson, trans. and ed., "Documents Relating to Peter Cassel and the Settlement at New Sweden," *Swedish American Historical Bulletin*, 2 (1929), 47–49. On Gasmann's account, see Nils Runeby, *Den nya världen och den gamla*, Studia Historica Upsaliensia, 30 (Uppsala: Svenska Bokförlaget, 1969), pp. 193–94, 203.
5. See G. N. Swan, "Staten Iowas första svenskar," Swedish Historical Society of America, *Yearbook*, 9 (1923–24), 40 (which does, however, note that the Anderssons came from Odensvi); George T. Flom, "Early Swedish Immigration to Iowa," *Iowa Journal of History and Politics*, 3 (1905), 602; Ardith K. Melloh, "New Sweden, Iowa," *Palimpsest*, 59 (1978), 5. To complicate matters, Peter Andersson has been confused in various sources with a later emigrant, Anders Peter Andersson (born 1809 in Odensvi), probably because he so soon left the Cassel colony in Iowa. Cf. Emil Lund, *Iowa-Konferensens af Augustana-Synoden historia* (Rock Island, Ill.: Augustana Book Concern, 1916), p. 648.
6. Stephenson, "Documents," p. 6, n. 1; Olsson, *Swedish Passenger Arrivals in New York*, pp. 64–67.

7. On Granschoug and Odensviholm manor, see Gun Willstadius et al., *Slott och herresäten i Sverige. Småland jemte Öland och Gotland* (Malmö: Allhem, 1971), pp. 344–48.

8. Olsson, *Swedish Passenger Arrivals in New York*, pp. 33, 64.

9. A. F. Cassel, "History of the First Swedish Emigrants in the 19th Century," speech for the fiftieth anniversary of New Sweden, 13 September 1895, as quoted in Carl J. Bengston, "The Early History of New Sweden, Iowa," Pt. I, manuscript in archives of the Lutheran Church in America, Chicago. Provided by Mrs. Lilly Setterdahl, East Moline, Illinois. Cf. the report on the anniversary and A. F. Cassel's speech in the *Fairfield Ledger* (Fairfield, Iowa), 18 September 1895, p. 3.

10. See, for instance, the accounts by Lars Paul Esbjörn from 1849, in my *Letters from the Promised Land*, pp. 46–52; Peterson, "From Östergötland to Iowa," pp. 146–50; [Eric Norelius], *Early Life of Eric Norelius, 1833–1862*, trans. Emeroy Johnson (Rock Island, Ill.: Augustana Book Concern, 1934), pp. 96–117. Also Moberg's novel, *The Emigrants*.

11. On Olof Hedström (from Småland), who first came to America in 1826, and his brother Jonas, who arrived in 1833, see Olsson, *Swedish Passenger Arrivals in New York*, pp. 12–13; Eric Norelius, *De svenska luterska församlingarna och svenskarnes historia i Amerika*, 2 vols. (Rock Island, Ill.: Augustana Book Concern, 1890, 1916), I, 16–26. On Olof Olsson, see Wesley M. Wesberberg, "Bethel Ship to Bishop Hill: Document (Letter of Olof Olsson)," *Swedish Pioneer Historical Quarterly*, 23 (1972), 55–70.

12. See Eric Corey, "New Sweden, Iowa," *Svenska Amerikanaren* (Chicago), 10 April 1930, p. 9 (series continued on 17 and 24 April 1930, in Swedish); C. L. Dahlberg and R. N. Dahlberg, "Pehr Dahlberg and the First Swedish Settlers in Iowa," *Annals of Iowa*, 3rd ser., 16 (1928), 323–30. Cf. Lilly Setterdahl, "Peter Cassels Amerika," manuscript, forthcoming in *Kisa sockenbok*, III, and in English as "Peter Cassel's America" in *Swedish Pioneer Historical Quarterly*.

13. A. F. Cassel, "History."

14. Setterdahl, "Peter Cassels Amerika."

15. Stephenson, "Documents," pp. 56–57. Cf. my *Letters from the Promised Land*, pp. 29–30.

16. Corey, "New Sweden, Iowa," *Svenska Amerikanaren*, 10 April 1930, p. 9.

17. Stephenson, "Documents," pp. 55–62. Cf. my *Letters from the Promised Land*, pp. 28–33.

18. Stephenson, "Documents," pp. 19–38 (in Swedish), pp. 51–72 (English translation); Per Cassel, *Beskrifning öfwer Amerikas Förenta Stater* (Westerwik: Tryckt hos E. O. Ekblad et Comp., 1846).

19. *Jönköpingsbladet* (Jönköping), 26 May 1846. Cf. Stephenson, "Documents," p. 2; my *Letters from the Promised Land*, p. 33.

20. Norelius, *De svenska luterska församlingarna*, I, 103–5, 116–17; Melloh, "New Sweden, Iowa," pp. 7–8.

21. See, for instance, the letter from Johan Farman of 15 May 1846,

published in *Östgöta Correspondenten*, 14 April 1847, Stephenson, "Documents," pp. 70–71.
22. Stephenson, "Documents," pp. 75–76. (Printed in *Östgöta Correspondenten*, 7 and 14 July 1849.)
23. Setterdahl, "Peter Cassels Amerika"; Melloh, "New Sweden, Iowa," p. 8.
24. Corey, "New Sweden, Iowa," *Svenska Amerikanaren*, 10 April 1930, p. 9. See also Melloh, "New Sweden, Iowa," pp. 8, 12–13.
25. Flom, "The Early Swedish Immigration to Iowa," pp. 611–12; Norelius, *De svenska luterska församlingarna*, I, 107–8; Lund, *Iowa-Konferensen*, p. 633; Helge Nelson, *The Swedes and the Swedish Settlements in North America*, 2 vols. (Lund: Gleerup, 1943), I, 252–53. Letter to me from Nils William Olsson, Sumner, Maryland, 30 March 1978; information from the manuscript of Dr. Olsson's forthcoming volume on Swedish passenger arrivals in American ports other than New York, 1820–50.
26. Norelius, *De svenska luterska församlingarna*, I, 107.
27. Setterdahl, "Peter Cassels Amerika." Little has been done thus far to trace the progressive establishment of daughter colonies of older Swedish settlements in North America. See, however, Nelson, *Swedes and Swedish Settlements*, esp. Map 12, Vol. II.
28. Ernst Skarstedt, *Oregon och Washington* (Portland, Ore.: Broström och Skarstedts Förlag, 1890), p. 250.
29. Norelius, *De svenska luterska församlingarna*, I, 107–8; Lund, *Iowa-Konferensen*, pp. 664–66.
30. Norelius, *De svenska luterska församlingarna*, I, 108. Also Lund, *Iowa-Konferensen*, p. 663.
31. Lund, *Iowa-Konferensen*, pp. 666, 670–71; Norelius, *De svenska luterska församlingarna*, I, 108.
32. Published by Western Historical Co., Chicago (p. 648). This source also states that although Fagerstrom first came to America in 1846, he did not actually settle in Polk Township until 1851. The apparent contradiction to other evidence may perhaps be explained by an absence from the township for a time between 1847 and 1851, when he probably acquired land there for the first time. I am obliged to Ardith K. Melloh for excerpts from this source. (Letter to me, Iowa City, 28 March 1978.) Also letter to me from Nils William Olsson, Sumner, Md., 30 March 1978, on census of 1850.
33. Norelius, *De svenska luterska församlingarna*, I, 108; Skarstedt, *Oregon och Washington*, p. 250.
34. Obituaries for Emma Christina Johnson, *Korsbaneret 1934* (Rock Island, Ill.: Augustana Book Concern), p. 281; for Gustaf Johnson, *Korsbaneret 1910*, pp. 233–34.
35. See Paul Elmen, *Wheat Flour Messiah* (Carbondale and Edwardsville: Southern Illinois University Press, 1976); Olov Isaksson and Sören Hallgren, *Bishop Hill: A Utopia on the Prairie* (Stockholm: LTs Förlag; Chicago: Swedish Pioneer Historical Society, 1969).

36. Ernst W. Olson, Anders Schön, and Martin J. Engberg, *History of the Swedes of Illinois*, 2 vols. (Chicago: Engberg-Holmberg Publ. Co., 1908), I, 371–81; Norelius, *De svenska luterska församlingarna*, I, 114–73; George M. Stephenson, *The Religious Aspects of Swedish Immigration* (Minneapolis: University of Minnesota Press, 1932), pp. 147–66; Erwin Weber, *Jenny Lind Chapel* (Rock Island, Ill.: Augustana College Library, 1975).
37. Obituaries for Gustaf and Emma Christina Johnson, *Korsbaneret* 1910 and 1934; obituary for Victor Nelson (Frans Viktor Nilsson), *Fort Dodge Messenger and Chronicle*, 7 February 1918.
38. Letter to me from Karin Augustinson, Ödeshög, 23 November 1976.

4. One of Nature's Americans

1. The following account of Örhn's life in Sweden, his own and the Hornwall families, is based, unless otherwise noted, on information from church and property records preserved at Vadstena *landsarkiv*, in letters to me from: Sven Malmberg, Vadstena, 22 June 1972, 7 February 1974; Nils William Olsson, Molkom, 26 July, 2 September 1972; Maja Nestor, Gullringen, 27 September 1973; Karin Augustinson, Ödeshög, 28 September 1973, 27 November, 7 December 1974, 13 February, 7 July 1975.
2. Gamleby (="Old Town") was on the original site of Västervik, which was reestablished at its present location following a fire in 1433.
3. Letter to me from Sune Garpenby, Gamleby, 25 February 1974.
4. Letter to me from Elsa Larsson, Odensvi, February 1974.
5. From Karin Augustinson's research notes on Jonas Öhrn.
6. See Lund, *Iowa-Konferensen*, pp. 652–55.
7. Letter to me from Elsa Larsson, Odensvi, February 1976.
8. "History of the Church," from the commemorative program booklet for the ninetieth anniversary of the New Sweden Methodist Church, 14–16 June 1940, p. 7.
9. Olsson, *Swedish Passenger Arrivals in New York*, pp. 180, 181.
10. Letter to me from Kevin Proescholdt, Ames, Iowa, 9 September 1976. Mr. Proescholdt wrote his senior honors thesis at Iowa State University on "New Sweden, Iowa: A Narrative History," using census materials. See also Olsson, *Swedish Passenger Arrivals in New York*, pp. 180, 181.
11. Norelius, *De svenska luterska församlingarna*, I, 87–97; Lund, *Iowa-Konferensen*, pp. 651, 661.
12. Victor Witting, *Minnen från mitt lif* (Worcester, Mass.: Burbank och Co:s Tryckeri, 1904), pp. 214–15; Lund, *Iowa-Konferensen*, p. 653.
13. See, for instance, the description of religious dissension in a Norwegian prairie community in Ole Rølvaag's novel, *Peder Victorious* (New York: Harper and Bros., 1929).

14. On New Sweden's population, see "New Sweden, Iowa," in *Hemlandet, det Gamla och det Nya* (Galesburg, Ill.), 30 March 1858, p. 1.
15. See Stephenson, *Religious Aspects*, Ch. 3.
16. *Hemlandet*, 30 March 1858, p. 1. The newspaper moved to Chicago at the end of the year. See also Norelius, *De svenska luterska församlingarna*, I, 97–99; Nelson, *Swedes and Swedish Settlements*, I, 250–51; Kevin Proescholdt's research notes. (See n. 10, above.)
17. "History of the Church" (New Sweden Methodist), pp. 9–10.
18. Norelius, *De svenska luterska församlingarna*, I, 101. Cf. Nelson, *Swedes and Swedish Settlements*, I, 251.
19. Both were among the first group of settlers in 1845 and were fellow Methodists. The will is on file at the Jefferson County Courthouse, Fairfield. In her letter to me of 7 July 1975, Karin Augustinson informs me that Öhrn was literate, according to Odensvi parish records.
20. A classic statement of this view is Oscar Handlin's *The Uprooted* (New York: Grosset and Dunlap, 1951), which is based primarily upon the model of the late nineteenth-century eastern European emigrant.
21. See Sten Carlsson, "Flyttningsintensiteten i det svenska agrarsamhället," *Turun historiallinen arkisto*, 28 (1973), 189–210. (Includes English summary.)
22. George M. Stephenson, "The Attitude of Swedish Americans toward the World War," *Mississippi Valley Historical Association Proceedings*, 10, No. 1 (1918–19), 93.

5.   The Master of Bullebo

1. The legal agreement for the property division and a map showing the new property lines is in the possession of Nils Olsson, Bullebo. Details on Bullebo from letter to me from Sven Malmberg, Vadstena, 22 June 1972.
2. Oral information provided by Erik Karlsson, Djursdala, in 1966.
3. Moberg, *The Emigrants*, p. 9.
4. Florence E. Janson, *The Background of Swedish Immigration, 1840–1930* (University of Chicago Press, 1931), pp. 75–77, 151, 222–25. See also Sigfrid Svensson, *Från gammalt till nytt på 1800-talets svenska landsbygd* (Stockholm: LTs förlag, 1977), esp. pp. 47–55. It is estimated that land reclamation almost tripled the amount of Sweden's cultivated land between 1800 and 1860. (Gustav Sundbärg, *Emigrationsutredningen. Betänkande* [Stockholm: Norstedt, 1913], p. 91.)
5. Letters to me from Gösta Karlsson, Djursdala, 11 March, 22 October 1972; conversation with same, August 1973; letter to me from Fru Eddy Gustafsson, Vimmerby, 16 July 1972.
6. Conversation with Fru Eddy Gustafsson, Vimmerby, August 1973.
7. On land reallocations, the breakup of villages, and their social effects, see Eli F. Heckscher, *Sveriges ekonomiska historia från Gustaf Vasa*, 4 vols. (Stockholm: Bonnier, 1935–49), II, Pt. I, 247–83; Ingers

and Carlsson, *Bonden i svensk historia*, II, 461–502, III, 11–116; B. J. Hovde, *The Scandinavian Countries, 1720–1865*, 2 vols. (Boston, Chapman and Grimes, 1943), I, Chs. 3, 7.

8. Janson, *Background of Swedish Immigration*, pp. 222–25.
9. Letter to me from Eddy Gustafsson, Vimmerby, 16 July 1972.
10. [Nelson], *Swedish Settlements in Iowa*, p. 51; letters to me from Gösta Karlsson, Djursdala, 13 July 1972; from Clifford Swenson, Gowrie, 3 February 1972.
11. John T. Svenson, Gowrie, to Emil Carlsson, Djursdala, 4 December 1930.
12. Letter to me from Eddy Gustafsson, Vimmerby, 16 July 1972; John T. Svenson to Emil Carlsson, Gowrie, 8 September 1929, 22 March 1930.
13. Stephenson, *Religious Aspects*, Ch. 3.
14. Elis Stig, "Skolhistoria från Södra Vi," *Södra Vi-krönikan*, 3 (1967), 10–19.
15. Bygdén, *Härnösands stifts herdaminnen*, I, 67; [Nelson], *Swedish Settlements in Iowa*, p. 51; O. Fritiof Ander, *T. N. Hasselquist* (Rock Island, Ill.: Augustana Book Concern, 1931), p. 213; Albin Widén, "Från Sverige-Fronten," *Nordstjernan-Svea* (New York), 16 December 1971, pp. 4, 8.
16. Stephenson, *Religious Aspects*, Chs. 11, 12.
17. See Gunnar Westin, ed., *Emigranterna och kyrkan* (Stockholm: Svenska kyrkans diakonistyrelses bokförlag, 1932), pp. 326–27, 335–37, letters given in English translation in my *Letters from the Promised Land*, pp. 157–60, showing the enthusiasm of Ahlberg's pupils to serve in America.
18. John T. Svenson to Emil Carlsson, Gowrie, 8 September 1929.
19. Letter to me from Gösta Karlsson, Djursdala, 26 February 1972.
20. John T. Svenson to Emil Carlsson, Gowrie, 4 December 1930.
21. John T. Svenson to Emil Carlsson, Gowrie, 20 January 1932.
22. Leonard Carlsson, "Några märkliga Södra Vi-bor," *Södra Vi-krönikan*, I (1960), 8.
23. Stephenson, "Documents," pp. 3n., 12n., 62n. There are indications of family connections with Örsåsa since at least 1745. (Letters to me from Karin Augustinson, Ödeshög, 14 February 1976, 6 October 1977.) George M. Stephenson, ed. and trans., "An America Letter of 1849," Swedish Historical Society of America, *Yearbook*, 9 (1926), 84–102.
24. Olsson, *Swedish Passenger Arrivals in New York*, p. 165. He was Pehr Svensson—no relative of Sven Svensson.
25. Letters to me from Sven Malmberg, Vadstena, 22 June 1972; from Karin Augustinson, Ödeshög, 14 February 1976.
26. Total Swedish immigration to America in 1867 was 5,893 persons; in 1868 it was 21,472, and in 1869, 32,053. Emigration from Djursdala parish was 28 in 1867 and 62 in 1868. (Summarisk redogörelse.)
27. For such a scene, see Peterson, "From Östergötland to Iowa,"

pp. 139–41; also reprinted in my *Letters from the Promised Land*, pp. 54–55. See also Moberg, *The Emigrants*, Ch. 10, Pt. 2.
28. Letter to me from Eddy Gustafsson, Vimmerby, 16 July 1972. A basically similar version is contained in a letter to me from Gösta Karlsson, Djursdala, 11 March 1972. My father recalled hearing during his visit to Djursdala in 1960 that Sven's prayer went: "May no one who swears, plays cards, or indulges in other works of the Devil live here."

6. Fresh Beginnings on the Prairie

1. On travel to America, see Philip Taylor, *The Distant Magnet* (New York: Torchbooks-Harper, 1971), Chs. 7–8. On the activities of a typical steamship agency, see Berit Brattne, "The Larsson Brothers: A Study of the Activity of Swedish Emigrant Agencies During the 1880's," *American Studies in Scandinavia*, 9 (Winter 1972), 31–51. For Johan August Nilsson and family, letter to me from Karin Augustinson, Ödeshög, 23 November 1976.
2. For travel accounts by Swedish emigrants on this route in this period, see, for instance, Johannes V. Swenson, "A Journey from Sweden to Texas 90 Years Ago," *Swedish Pioneer Historical Quarterly*, 8 (1957), 128–35, reprinted in my *Letters from the Promised Land*, pp. 121–26; Alan Swanson, trans. and ed., "'Some Cried and Some Sang . . .' The Emigrant Journal of Peter Johan Jönsson," *Swedish Pioneer Historical Quarterly*, 26 (1975), 157–84. Some Swedish emigrants sailed from Christiania, Copenhagen, Hamburg, Bremen, and other ports. A few still seem to have sailed directly from Swedish ports. The *Wimmerby Weckotidning* (Vimmerby) for 31 May 1867 noted the departure from nearby Oscarshamn of the steamship *Bråwiken* for "America" with 196 emigrants, on 23 May—less than a month before the Svenssons left Djursdala.
3. My *Letters from the Promised Land*, pp. 109, 137.
4. Ibid., pp. 108–9.
5. See Ch. 3, above. Obituary for Victor Nelson, *Fort Dodge Messenger and Chronicle*, 7 February 1918; E. Olson, *Swedes of Illinois*, I, 321–24; H. Nelson, *Swedes and Swedish Settlements*, I, 166.
6. E. Olson, *Swedes of Illinois*, I, 322–24.
7. [Nelson], *Swedish Settlements in Iowa*, pp. 41–43; Gustaf Burgh, "Reminiscences of an Iowa Pioneer," *Swedish Pioneer Historical Quarterly*, 6 (1955), 19. See also *Lost Grove Township, Webster County, Iowa, 1869–1969* (n.p., n.d.); Webster County Bicentennial Commission, *Webster's Prairies: The Township History of the County* (n.p., 1976).
8. Lund, *Iowa-Konferensen*, pp. 538–39.
9. [Nelson], *Swedish Settlements in Iowa*, p. 50; Burgh, "Reminiscences," p. 20.
10. Obituaries for Sara Maria Svenson in *Hemlandet* (Chicago), 18

August 1888, and for Sven Svenson, in *Iowa-Posten* (Des Moines), 14 August 1908. O. M. Nelson, in *Swedish Settlements in Iowa*, p. 51, claims that Sven moved his family from Altona to his farm in Lost Grove Township in 1869. Oscar's recollection from conversation with Marie Anderson, September 1973.

11. [Armanis F. Patton], "Lost Grove History," *Gowrie News*, 15 May 1952. Mr. Patton wrote this historical sketch evidently during the early 1930s.

12. Ibid.; Burgh, "Reminiscences," pp. 19–21.

13. Conversation with Marie Anderson, September 1973.

14. [Nelson], *Swedish Settlements in Iowa*, p. 51; [Patton], "Lost Grove History," *Gowrie News*, 15 May 1952; "The Story of Gowrie," Centennial Souvenir Edition, *Gowrie News*, 1 July 1970 (unpaginated); Lund, *Iowa-Konferensen*, pp. 539–41; conversation with Clifford Swenson, September 1973.

15. [Nelson], *Swedish Settlements in Iowa*, pp. 5, 41–42; H. Nelson, *Swedes and Swedish Settlements*, I, 254.

7. Forerunners

1. *Index to Compiled Service Records of Volunteer Union Soldiers Who Served in Organizations from the State of Illinois*, U.S. National Archives Microfilm Publication M 539; enlistment contract, in service record for Pvt. Ludvig Swanson, National Archives, Washington, D.C.

2. Stephenson, "Documents," p. 12n.; Olsson, *Swedish Passenger Arrivals in New York*, pp. 76–77, 165, 229, 231; George M. Stephenson, "An America Letter of 1849," Swedish Historical Society of America, *Yearbook*, 11 (1926), 87, 94; E. Olson, *Swedes of Illinois*, I, 275–77; Charles H. Hofland, "From Djursdala to Andover, Illinois, in 1850," *Swedish Pioneer Historical Quarterly*, 22 (1971), 34–44.

3. E. Olson, *Swedes of Illinois*, I, 626–27, 632–43; Nels Hokanson, *Swedish Immigrants in Lincoln's Time* (New York: Harper and Bros., 1942), pp. 68–77, 202; Nels Nelson, "Swedish-American Boys in Blue: Reminiscences from the Civil War," *Prärieblomman 1908* (Rock Island, Ill.: Augustana Book Concern, 1908), pp. 170–87.

4. See Hokanson, *Swedish Immigrants*, esp. pp. 52–67. On Hasselquist, see Ander, *T. N. Hasselquist*.

5. [Patton], "Lost Grove History," *Gowrie News*, 15 May 1952; "The Story of Gowrie," *Gowrie News*, 1 July 1970; Ludvig Svenson to parents, Des Moines, 1 February 1876.

6. [Nelson], *Swedish Settlements in Iowa*, p. 51.

7. Obituary for Joseph H. Nelson, May 1953, from unidentified newspaper, provided by Clifford Swenson, Gowrie.

8. Ander, *T. N. Hasselquist*, pp. 53–77, 213.

9. S. F. Westerdal to T. N. Hasselquist, Galesburg, 10 August 1866, Hasselquist Letter Collection (microfilm), Archives of the Lutheran Church in America, Chicago (hereafter abbreviated LCA). The originals

of these letters are in the Denkmann Memorial Library, Augustana College, Rock Island, Ill.

10. A. W. Dahlsten to T. N. Hasselquist, Galesburg, 10 August 1866, LCA.

11. T. N. Hasselquist to S. F. Westerdal, Paxton, 14 August 1866, LCA. On Hasselquist's policy of recommendations and admissions, see also T. N. Hasselquist to C. Carlsvärd, 30 August 1866, LCA.

12. T. N. Hasselquist to A. W. Dahlsten, 15 August 1866, LCA. Cf. Ander, T. N. Hasselquist, p. 64.

13. H. Olson to T. N. Hasselquist, New Sweden, Ia., 8 March 1867; T. N. Hasselquist to H. Olson, 22 March 1867; S. F. Westerdal to T. N. Hasselquist, 16 April 1867: LCA.

14. S. G. Larson to T. N. Hasselquist, 9 October 1867; B. M. Halland to T. N. Hasselquist, 18 February 1868; H. Olson to T. N. Hasselquist, 10 March 1868: LCA. Cf. the reminiscences of Olson's daughter from July 1943, in Albin Widén, Amerikaemigrationen i dokument (Stockholm: Prisma, 1966), pp. 126–27.

15. T. N. Hasselquist to H. Olson, 14 March 1868, LCA.

16. P. A. Cederstam to T. N. Hasselquist, 11 July 1869, 3 January 1870; E. Norelius to T. N. Hasselquist, 20 August 1869, 3 January 1870; S. F. Westerdal to T. N. Hasselquist, 3 February 1870, 16 September 1873; T. N. Hasselquist to E. Norelius, 21 July 1869, 12 February 1870: LCA. Cf. Eric Norelius, Vasa Illustrata. En borgerlig och kyrklig historia (Rock Island, Ill.: Augustana Book Concern, 1905), esp. p. 217; Emeroy Johnson, Eric Norelius (Rock Island, Ill.: Augustana Book Concern, 1954), pp. 149, 179; Albin Widén, Vår sista folkvandring (Stockholm: Geber, 1962), p. 111.

17. S. F. Westerdal to T. N. Hasselquist, 25 May 1871, 16 September 1873, LCA; Bygdén, Härnösands stifts herdaminnen, I, 68.

18. S. F. Westerdal to T. N. Hasselquist, 16 September, 18 November 1873, LCA.

19. Ibid.; T. N. Hasselquist to S. F. Westerdal, 3 October 1873, LCA.

20. Bygdén, Härnösands stifts herdaminnen, I, 67–68; Lund, Iowa-Konferensen, p. 547; biographical card file on pastors of the Augustana Synod, LCA.

8.   A Window into the Past

1. Letter to me from Registrar, Iowa State University, Ames, 7 April 1978. In January 1876 Victor Nelson borrowed stored seed wheat belonging to John. Victor to John, 8 January 1876. Much of my information on John Svenson, where not otherwise credited, derives from conversations with his grandson, Clifford Swenson, Gowrie.

2. Letters to John from Sven Svenson, 10 November, 20 December 1875, 14 January 1876; from Victor, 8 November 1875, 8 January 1876; L. D. Swainson [Ludvig] to parents, Des Moines, 1 February 1876.

3. Letters from Victor, 8 November 1875, 8 January, 23 March 1876;

from Ernest, 25 December 1875, 11, 27 February, 4 April 1876; from Tilda, 3 January, 22 February, 24 May, 16 June 1876.

4. Letters from Victor, 23 March, 26 April 1876; from Oscar, 6 May 1876; from Tilda, 16 June 1876.

5. Letters from Carolina Larson, 17 March, 29 May 1876.

6. Letters from Ernest, 1 August, 28 December 1876; from Carolina Larson, 10 September 1876; from W. A. White, 3 October 1876; from E. Nystrom, 2 October 1876; from N. Johnson, 4 November 1876; from S. F. Westerdal, 17 October, 21 December 1876.

7. Obituary for John T. Svenson, *Gowrie News*, 25 May 1933; John to Emil Carlsson in Djursdala, 21 March 1930; Clifford Swenson to me, Gowrie, 8 September 1976.

8. Letters from S. F. Westerdal, 3 July, 17 October, 21 December 1876.

9. Letters from Tilda, 3 January, 2 February, 22 March, 24 May, 16 June, 1876.

10. Letters from Sven Svenson, 10 November, 20 December 1875; from Irving, 19 January, 3, 7, 19 April 1876, 24 October 1877. The Augustana College catalog for 1875–76 lists him under the Preparatory Department.

11. Letters from Ernest, 25 December 1875, 11, 27 February, incomplete and undated [around March], 4, 20 April, 15 May, 21 June, 1 August, 13 November, 28 December 1876. The Augustana College catalog for 1877–78, 1878–79. Cf. Daniel M. Pearson, *The Americanization of Carl Aaron Swensson* Augustana Historical Society Publications, 25 (Rock Island, Ill., 1977).

12. Letters from Oscar, 20 December 1875, 6 May 1876; notes from Frida, 10 November 1875, and from Emil, 20 December 1875.

13. Letters from Ernest, 4 April 1876; from S. F. Westerdal, 3 July 1876.

9. The Family Goes Its Ways

1. On the early history of the Gowrie congregation, see Lund, *Iowa-Konferensen*, pp. 538–41; *Minnes-skrift utgifven af svenska ev. lutherska Gowrie-församlingen, Gowrie, Iowa* (Rock Island, Ill.: Augustana Book Concern, 1921); *Zion Lutheran Church, Gowrie, Iowa: Centennial Booklet* (Gowrie, Ia., 1971); "The Story of Gowrie," *Gowrie News*, 1 July 1970. Also M. C. Ranseen to T. N. Hasselquist, West Dayton, Ia., 22 August 1871; John Teleen to T. N. Hasselquist, Des Moines, 26 August 1872: LCA.

2. Letters to John from Victor, 8 January 1876; from Ernest, 20 April 1876.

3. Lund, *Iowa-Konferensen*, pp. 541–43; *Minnes-skrift*, pp. 20–21; *Zion Lutheran Church*; "The Story of Gowrie," *Gowrie News*, 1 July 1970; S. F. Westerdal to T. N. Hasselquist, 24 March 1880, LCA. Cf. Widén, *Vår sista folkvandring*, pp. 106–7.

4. Bygdén, *Härnösands stifts herdaminnen*, I, 68; conversation with Marie Anderson, September 1973.

5. Lund, *Iowa-Konferensen*, p. 542.

6. Card file on pastors of the Augustana Lutheran Church, LCA; Bygdén, *Härnösands stifts herdaminnen*, I, 68; letter to me from Karin Augustinson, Ödeshög, 7 December 1974, containing information from Fru Elsa Ekberg, Uppsala. On New Sweden, Maine, see W. W. Thomas, Jr., "The Story of New Sweden," *Collections and Proceedings of the Maine Historical Society*, 2nd. ser., 7 (1896).

7. Declaration for Invalid Pension, 11 December 1900; Ludvig D. Swainson to Messrs. John W. Morris and Co., Cripple Creek, Colo., 25 November 1906; declarations for pension, 9 March 1907, 13 May 1914, National Archives, Washington, D.C.; Ernest to John, Portland, Ore., 26 December 1903; conversation with Marie Anderson, January 1976.

8. See "The Story of Gowrie," *Gowrie News*, 1 July 1970, which provides much detail on the establishment and transfer of the community's businesses and includes a picture of its first, eleven-man band.

9. Ellen Watkins to Margit McNulty, Fort Dodge [18] December 1957.

10. "The Story of Gowrie," *Gowrie News*, 1 July 1970; letter to me from Crayton M. Watkins, Jr., Burbank, Calif., 9 December 1974. On the antipathy between the Scandinavians and the Irish, see Ole Rølvaag's novel, *Peder Victorious*.

11. Letter to me from Clifford Swenson, Gowrie, 3 February 1972; photograph of Dr. and Mrs. C. E. Lundgren, dated Christmas 1879.

12. Letter to me from Clifford Swenson, Gowrie, 3 February 1972; conversation with Marie Anderson, September 1973.

13. Conversation with Marie Anderson, September 1973. Maria Charlotta Andersson [Löfstedt] was born in Värmland.

14. "The Story of Gowrie," *Gowrie News*, 1 July 1970; conversations with Clifford Swenson and Marie Anderson, 1973, 1976. Concerning one of Gowrie's daughter colonies, see the letter from C. A. Liljegren to John Svenson, Stockholm, Kansas (*not* South Dakota), 30 December 1892, in my *Letters from the Promised Land*, pp. 221–22.

15. Skarstedt, *Oregon och Washington*, p. 229. My copy of this book was given me in 1973 by Clifford Swenson, and had doubtless been given by Ernest to John and family. Ernest to niece, 19 December 1922; Ernest to Theodore Svenson, 15 February 1888.

16. Ernest to Theodore Svenson, Omaha, 15 February, 10 March 1888; Oscar to Theodore, Omaha, 17 March 1892; [C. E.] Lundgren to parents-in-law, St. Paul, 8 January 1883.

17. On Jenny Norelius, see Gustaf Toll, "Bollnäsflickan som blev storsångerska i USA," *Allsvensk samling*, 40 (June 1953), 10–12. A good deal is preserved on her and her career in newspapers and musical journals, which I hope to make use of.

18. Marriage certificate dated 15 January 1890; Skarstedt, *Oregon och Washington*, p. 229.

19. Ibid., p. 228.

20. Ernest to John, North Yamhill, Ore., 3 January 1895.
21. Skarstedt, *Oregon och Washington*, p. 229.
22. Discussion with my father, March 1972.
23. Karin Augustinson to me, Ödeshög, 28 September 1973, 29 October 1976.

10. The Passing of an Era

1. Notation in John Svenson's Bible, in possession of Clifford Swenson; conversation with Marie Anderson, January 1976.
2. Obituary for Sara Marie Svenson, *Hemlandet* (Chicago), 18 August 1888.
3. Härnösand cathedral chapter to the king, 27 April 1892, with attached testimonials, Ecklesiastikdepartementets arkiv, Riksarkivet, Stockholm.
4. Bygdén, *Härnösands stifts herdaminnen*, I, 67–68; letter to me from Karin Augustinson, Ödeshög, 21 May 1974.
5. Ernest to John, North Yamhill, Ore., 3 January 1895. On the relations between the Swedish state church and the Augustana Lutheran Synod, see Stephenson, *Religious Aspects*. A few years after Sven Fredrik's death, in 1906, there were thirty-five pastors from the Augustana Synod serving the state church in Sweden. (Ander, *T. N. Hasselquist*, pp. 223–24.)
6. Sven David Westerdal to John, Karsnäs, Södra Vi, 22 February 1903.
7. Letters to me from Karin Augustinson, Ödeshög, 21 May, 27 November, 7 December 1974. Karin Augustinson learned a number of details from Fru Ester Ekberg of Uppsala, a second cousin to Mathilda and Ida Björkman. Conversation with Marie Anderson, September 1976.
8. Ellen Watkins to Margit McNulty, Fort Dodge [Christmas 1961]; conversation with Marie Anderson, September 1973.
9. Conversation with Marie Anderson, September 1973.
10. Conversations with Clifford Swenson and Marie Anderson, September 1973; Ernest to John, Portland, 4, 26 April, 18 May 1903. Marie Anderson still possesses ten acres and her son Kermit a little over one acre of the old Svenson property.
11. Conversation with Marie Anderson, September 1973; notice in *Iowa-Posten* (Des Moines), 7 August 1908; obituary, ibid., 14 August 1908.
12. Pension records for Ludvig D. Swainson, National Archives, Washington, D.C.; Ernest to John, Portland, 26 December 1903; letter to me from Clifford Swenson, Gowrie, 3 February 1972; conversation with Marie Anderson, January 1976.
13. [C. E.] Lundgren to parents-in-law, St. Paul, 8 January 1883; letter to me from Clifford Swenson, 3 February 1972. The photographs of the Roseberry family, found among my grandmother's effects, had

probably been sent originally to Frida. The current edition of *Burke's Peerage* shows that some members of the Rosebery family settled in western Canada by the end of the nineteenth century.

14. Murray, Hollaman, and Lockwood, Lawyers, to John, New York, 29 September 1921; Margit McNulty to me, North Hollywood, Calif., 2 March 1972.

15. Margit McNulty to me, North Hollywood, 2 March 1972, Laguna Hills, Calif., 5 February 1976.

16. Ernest to John, Loomis, Wash., 21 November 1914; Frida to John, Seattle, 4 June, aboard S.S. *Victoria*, 9 June, undated [Nome, June] 1916, Solomon, Alaska, 29 August 1917; Linda Rose McCabe, "Home-Making in the Yukon," *Eagle Magazine* (August 1916), pp. 5–6; Gösta Karlsson to me, Djursdala, 3 September 1972. It is possible that the visitor to Djursdala might have been Tilda.

17. Frida to John, Nome, 6 August 1919.

18. Frida to John, Seattle, 1 March 1923; Mrs. George Pullen to Sophie Nelson, Gresham, Ore., 12 August, 4 September 1925; Ellen Watkins to Margit McNulty, Fort Dodge, 17 December 1957; Crayton M. Watkins, Jr., to me, Burbank, Calif., 19 December 1974; Margit McNulty to me, North Hollywood, 2 March 1972.

19. Ernest to John, Portland, 1 February 1893.

20. Ernest to John, Andover, 1 August 1876.

21. Information from my father; Margit McNulty to me, Laguna Hills, 5 February 1976; conversation with Marie Anderson, September 1976.

22. Ernest to John, North Yamhill, 3 January 1895, 21 October 1896. On the Swedish Lutherans' tendency to equate godliness with Republicanism, see Ander, *T. N. Hasselquist*, pp. 205–7.

23. Ernest to John, North Yamhill, 21 October 1896; Jenny to Hildor, Seattle, 20 October 1924.

24. Information from my father; Margit McNulty to me, North Hollywood, 2 March 1972.

25. Ernest to John, North Yamhill, 3 January 1895.

26. Conversations with my father, March 1972; with Margit McNulty, December 1973. On Skarstedt, see Emory Lindquist, *An Immigrant's American Odyssey: A Biography of Ernst Skarstedt*, Augustana Historical Society Publications, 24 (Rock Island, Ill., 1974).

27. Conversation with my father, March 1972; Margit McNulty to me, North Hollywood, 2 March 1972, Laguna Hills, 26 June 1976. See also Emmett A. Greenwalt, *The Point Loma Experiment in California, 1897–1942* (Berkeley: University of California Press, 1955).

28. Ernest to John, North Yamhill, 3 January 1895.

29. Ernest to John, Portland, 4 April 1902.

30. Ernest to John, Portland, 26 April, 18 May 1903.

31. Clifford Swenson to me, Gowrie, 3 January 1972.

32. Ernest to John, North Yamhill, 3 January 1895; Margit McNulty to me, North Hollywood, 17 February 1972, Laguna Hills, 5 February, 26 June 1976; conversation with my father, March 1972. See Ernst

Skarstedt's poem in honor of Jenny's farewell recital in Portland on 30 June 1900, in his *Under vestliga skyar* (Tacoma, Wash.: På eget förlag, 1907), pp. 89–90. On Jenny's career, see Toll, "Bollnäsflickan."

33. Ernest to niece, 19 December 1922; Ernest to John, undated, 25 December 1903; conversations with my father; Margit McNulty to me, North Hollywood, 17 February 1972.

34. Ernest to John, Loomis, Wash., 21 November 1914; Jenny to Hildor, Seattle, 9 December 1920, 20, 27 October 1924; Margit McNulty to me, North Hollywood, 17 February, 2 March 1972, Laguna Hills, 5 February, 26 June 1976.

35. Ernest to niece, 19 December 1922; to Margit, Seattle, 19 November 1923.

36. Jenny to Hildor, Seattle, 20, 27 October 1924, 27 July 1925; to John, Seattle, 17 February 1926; Margit McNulty to me, North Hollywood, 2 March 1972.

37. Jenny to Hildor, Seattle, 27 October 1924; to John, Seattle, 17 February 1926; conversations with my father. I have in my possession a carton of plans and papers relating to the Forno smelter.

38. Ellen Watkins to Margit McNulty, Fort Dodge, 18 December 1957, undated [Christmas 1961]; Crayton M. Watkins, Jr., to me, Burbank, 9 December 1974; death certificate for Victor Nelson, dated 10 February 1918, Iowa State Department of Health, Division of Records and Statistics, Des Moines.

39. John to Emil Carlsson, Gowrie, 30 January 1932.

40. Eddy Gustafsson to me, Vimmerby, 16 July 1972.

41. John to Emil Carlsson, Göteborg, 21 September 1928, Gowrie, 20 January 1932; Emil Carlsson to John, Bullebo, 17 November 1928.

42. John to Emil Carlsson, Gowrie, 21 September, 18 October, 17 November 1928, 8 September 1929, 21–22 March, 18 April, 4 December 1930, 20 January, 24 March 1932.

43. [Patton], "Lost Grove History," *Gowrie News*, 15 May 1952; [Nelson], *Swedish Settlements in Iowa*, p. 51.

44. Obituary in *Gowrie News*, 25 May 1933.

45. Obituaries in the *Gowrie News*, 8 August 1935, and the *Fort Dodge Chronicle*, 3 August 1935. It is, of course, just possible that Tilda, the date of whose death is unknown, was the last of her generation to go.

11. Epilogue

1. Franklin D. Scott, "The 1974 Essay Contest," *Swedish Pioneer Historical Quarterly*, 26 (1976), 113.

2. For the Swedes, this viewpoint is most effectively maintained by Sture Lindmark, in *Swedish America, 1914–1932*, Studia Historica Upsaliensia, 37 (Uppsala: Läromedelsförlagen; Chicago: Swedish Pioneer Historical Society, 1971), and Ulf Beijbom, *Swedes in Chicago*, Studia Historica Upsaliensia, 38 (Uppsala: Läromedelsförlagen; Chicago: Chicago Historical Society, 1971). See also Robert S. Salisbury, "Swedish-

American Historiography and the Question of Americanization," *Swedish Pioneer Historical Quarterly*, 29 (1978), 117–36.

3. See Will Herberg, *Protestant, Catholic, Jew* (Garden City, N.Y.: Doubleday, 1956), which presents the concept of a "triple melting pot," following the major religious divisions in American society.

4. Quoted in Marc Bloch, *The Historian's Craft* (New York: Vintage-Random, 1964), p. 35.

5. Edmund Burke, *Reflections on the Revolution in France* (1790; rpt. New York: Gateway Editions, 1955), p. 140.

Index